Quiche & Pâté

PETER KUMP

ILLUSTRATED BY SUSAN GRAY

HARPER & ROW, PUBLISHERS, New York

Cambridge, Philadelphia, San Francisco, London

Mexico City, São Paulo, Sydney

IRENA CHALMERS COOKBOOKS, INC., New York

For Simca, Jim and Diana
No one had better teachers or finer friends

Any book of this nature represents a joint effort. The contents are pulled together by the author with the counsel of the editor. As a cooking teacher, my interests lie mainly in training students rather than in developing recipes, yet this book called for me to work out a number of new recipes and ideas as well as to adapt some old ones. It has been a grand experience, and I am indebted to Irena Chalmers for offering it to me. It has been wonderful to work with such a professional.

Ideas come from everywhere, and in the food world we often wonder whether there is truly anything new. My work has been heavily influenced by my teachers, whom I hope I have represented well, and it also draws from many other sources, which I have made an effort to acknowledge. My son Christopher assisted me by endlessly testing quiches and pâtés during a glorious Alpine summer when he would much rather have been out in the sun. My colleague Anabelle Vela helped me to finish the work in New York City in spite of our very heavy teaching load. And then there were the eaters. There have been many, some who even said they weren't tired of quiches after eating as many as five different ones a day for many days on end. They included Sherri Heller, Marty Sobin, Chris-Paul Stapels and my parents, who also obligingly made available their Austrian home, a medieval castle, where I could cook and write in solitude.

Both Simone Beck and James Beard read the manuscript and offered excellent comments and suggestions, for which I cannot adequately express my thanks. John Clancy hounded me unmercifully to write a cookbook, and this is it; the hounding was necessary, as anyone who has ever sat down and faced a blank piece of paper knows. My assistants in New York, Nora Bricke and Alexina Shufeldt, provided the needed support and help that gave me the time to do this work.

FIRST HARPER & ROW EDITION

Library of Congress Cataloging in Publication Data

Kump, Peter.
 Quiche & pâté.

 (Great American cooking schools series) 1. Quiches (Cookery) 2. Pâtés (Cookery) I. Title. II. Title: Quiche and pâté. III. Series.
TX773.K74 1982   641.8'2   82-47862
ISBN 0-06-015067-X

82 83 84 85 86 10 9 8 7 6 5 4 3 2 1

Contents

Pâté

About the Author

I came to teaching cooking in a roundabout way. Like James Beard and Julia Child, I'm from the West Coast. I grew up in what was then the country (Los Altos, California) on a small ranch which sported a vegetable garden that had just about everything known to Western gardeners of that time: a citrus orchard with lemon, orange, lime and grapefruit trees; a nut orchard with at least one tree of every variety that would grow in northern California; and a small vineyard (our one attempt at winemaking was not remarkable). We even raised chickens and occasionally ducks and turkeys, and there were a few steers which were slaughtered on the property. We always ate fresh food, well cooked in a very grand American style.

I vividly remember the first time my father went to Europe and came back with lavish tales of the magnificent meals he had eaten. I recall his asking my mother to make croissants. Her recipe must have come from *The Joy of Cooking*, which was her bible. The croissants were tiny and I don't remember that they were anything special, but I do remember my father's reassuring her that they were *almost* like the ones he had eaten in France. Mother is a fine cook, but though she is part French there was no appreciation of French cooking in her kitchen.

This was all to change when I was fifteen, when we moved to Europe for a year and I was suddenly thrust into a very different world. Though I remember crying at the thought of leaving my good friends for so long a time, I also remember that I loved going to school in French Switzerland. Among other reasons, I had never eaten so well, even though I was eating "institutional" food. When my family returned to the United States, I insisted upon staying, and did.

When I finally came home to go to Stanford, the shock of dormitory food was too much. As soon as I could, I moved off campus and began to cook for myself. My roommate, Fritz Maytag, was a willing accomplice; he hated to cook but got satisfaction from washing dishes, which he regarded as an opportunity for meditation. As I hated doing dishes, an agreement was struck and I quickly learned to cook.

At that time in my life my first love was the theater, and I formed a repertory company which I ran for a good many years in California. But all the good things I had learned to appreciate in Europe, good food among them, had no room in this gypsy life style. So I decided to return to school, this time to Carnegie-Mellon in Pittsburgh. To prepare myself, I took a speed-reading course, and when I was asked to teach the same course, I gladly accepted, to help pay my way through school. I discovered that I had a gift for teaching and that I enjoyed it as much as I enjoyed my work in the theater. I was working for Evelyn Wood, who really does exist, and who personally taught me something special: If the students haven't learned, you haven't taught. That maxim has always dominated my philosophy of teaching. I also discovered that learning didn't have to be dull and boring—it could and should be an exciting experience.

Eventually I moved to New York City and as a hobby began taking cooking courses, always seeking out the very best instructors. Simone Beck was my first teacher and we became friends. I ended up learning more from working at her side in her kitchen in southern France than I ever did in formal classes; I also learned to love Provence more than almost any other place. Next I got into a master's class with my idol, James Beard. We discovered that we were fellow alumni of the Carnegie drama department, and another close friendship was struck. I learned a tremendous amount from Jim, including how to conduct participation classes. He introduced me to many other cooks from whom I learned a great deal, and his fine palate—perhaps the most sensitive I've encountered in this country—led to a greater depth and awareness on my part.

I studied next with Diana Kennedy, who broadened my experience from a very different point of view and background. Not only is she extremely knowledgeable about Mexican cuisines, but she has an extraordinary talent for baking, not to mention a first-rate education in all Western cooking. Working at her side in New York and in Mexico, and developing a close friendship, provided me with a wealth of information, techniques and insights. Marcella Hazan, a very gifted woman, was another of my teachers. Though we have remained friends, I haven't had the opportunity to spend as much time with her and her husband, Victor, as I would like; it seems that we are always at opposite ends of the world at the same time. Of course there have been many other teachers, schools, courses, chefs I've observed and restaurants where I've helped out, here and in Europe, but these people have been the main influences on my work.

Meanwhile I was cooking away, always inspired by annual trips to Europe, especially to France, Italy and Austria. When several friends asked me to teach them to cook, I began to think

about how I would design the ideal course with the objective of helping students to learn in the shortest possible time all the tricks and techniques it had taken me years to acquire. After months of preparation I taught my first course. Diana Kennedy liked what I was doing; she felt that no one else in New York was teaching the basic fundamentals in this particular way, and she was very sensitive to the fact that many of her students didn't know the basics. She recommended to Mimi Sheraton of *The New York Times* that she should come to observe the classes, and apparently Mimi approved, because her good words are what really launched a teaching career that had begun only as a hobby.

Today there are several of us who teach at the school. The program that I developed in 1974 has held up well, requiring surprisingly few improvements, but four courses have been added so that the curriculum now comprises a survey of French cooking techniques. We attempt to offer professional-level classes to dedicated non-professionals who are able to attend only once a week. The classes are limited in size and involve complete participation. A technique is demonstrated, after which everyone has the opportunity to repeat it, because I don't believe that people learn unless they *do* something. (Of course there is also a place for demonstration classes: Once the students know the basic techniques, a demonstration class is actually more valuable because it allows them to see, taste and experience more than if they had to do all the work themselves. However, if they don't have the basic techniques, most of a demonstration is lost.)

Becoming a good cook requires several attributes and some of us have more of them than others. I think the first and most important thing is a sensitive and discriminating palate. Though this is hard to develop when one is older, almost like learning a language, it is possible. But you must expand your taste experiences and do so intelligently. If there is more than a handful of things that you don't like to eat, then you have a problem that I call crippled palate. (I find it odd that most Americans will say "I don't eat such-and-such" almost proudly. To me this is like admitting that one has never read some important book, knows nothing about it, and does not intend to find out.) My first suggestion to you when you are in a fine restaurant is not to waste your time ordering what you know you already like; order what you have never tried, and keep on trying new things.

The second important requirement for a good cook is technique. Knowing how things work and why, and what to do if something goes wrong all this is vital. These things certainly can be self-taught, but it is more efficient to go to a good school and learn them quickly. Profit by others' mistakes!

And finally, a cook needs to develop an extensive "vocabulary" of foods and their variations and subtle combinations. This also requires constant exposure to new things, and the seeking out of the untried.

All this is learnable and teachable, and what I most enjoy doing is trying to teach as much of it as possible in the shortest possible time. It's very exciting to me because the challenge never ends.

In this book I have tried to impart some of this way of teaching by beginning with a section that explains the fundamentals of making quiches, pastry and pâtés, and another that offers tips on ingredients and basic techniques. If you learn this information well, you should have no difficulty executing the recipes provided, and should soon be well on your way to creating your own.

I feel strongly that anyone who doesn't try to eat as well as possible is being deprived of one of life's greatest experiences. I hope that you learn to perform this daily miracle for yourself and that this small book helps you to enjoy those pleasures of living.

Introduction

Quiche (pronounced keesh) and pâté (pah-tay) have more in common than the fact that both, as we know them today, were developed in France. Both are primarily served as a first course, both use a kind of short pastry (*pâte brisée*, pronounced paht bree-zay) and both are currently popular in America. The words for these delicious foods have become part of the American vocabulary. With our usual inventiveness, we have begun to develop new ideas for quiches and pâtés and to stretch old ones.

Despite their popularity, quiches and pâtés have a way of intimidating cooks who are unfamiliar with them. But there are quiches that can be made in a pie plate in a matter of minutes by a novice. And several of the pâtés presented in this book are equally simple to execute and delicious to serve. But as a teacher, I hope that the most important contribution of this book will be a grasp of the cooking techniques which will enable you not only to tackle the most difficult recipes for quiches and pâtés, but to go on and make up your own with a solid understanding of these cooking foundations.

At the beginning of each of the two main sections is an introduction which provides information on the various techniques used, the general proportions to follow in making up your own recipes, cooking times, seasoning tips and such. Read these carefully and refer back to them when necessary. Directions in some of the easier recipes are more explicit than in the harder ones, which use procedures familiar to any cook who has made some of the easier dishes.

Quiches are excellent for last-minute execution if you have a quiche shell ready-baked and frozen. If you don't, use the Fear-of-Pastry Crust (page 31), which can be put together in seconds. Pâtés, on the other hand, vary considerably; there are several that can be made at the last minute, but traditional pâtés are usually cooked at least a day before eating, to allow the flavor to develop.

I am particularly pleased with the dessert quiches and terrines. Though dessert quiches would be called flans in France, these are definitely quiches from an American viewpoint. When I decided that I would like to include dessert pâtés, I wondered if anyone would think I was going a bit too far, but good counsel came from the French edition of the *Larousse Gastronomique*. Dessert pâtés used to exist, so I wasn't crazy to start working in that area. Only two are presented here, but once made they should re-open a whole new area for inventive cooks. And serving them seems right in the mainstream of the current vogue for nouvelle cuisine.

Be certain to read the ingredients and techniques sections carefully before using the recipes. No one can overcome inferior ingredients, and a good understanding of the basic techniques can help you avoid a lot of problems. Cooking is essentially a form of chemistry with an incredible number of variables. No matter what a cookbook specifies, no matter how clearly, someone reading it will find some ingredient that varies in some way from what is available in the local market, and the recipe will work in some new way—perhaps exciting, but not always—when ingredients or methods are changed. To be successful you must know what to look for—for example, how to tell when a dish is done even if, according to the instructions, it has another 20 minutes to go.

There is always controversy over measuring ingredients: some good cooks supposedly "don't," other experts insist upon it. My good friend James Beard brought the following passage to my attention. It's by Mrs. D. A. Lincoln, as printed in the 1883 edition of the *Boston Cookbook*:

It has been said that good cooks never measure anything. They do—they measure by judgment and experience. And until you have a large share of both these essential qualities, use your spoon and cup or scales.

Enjoy the recipes, both making them and eating them!

Tips on Ingredients
for Successful Results

It's very often the simplest of ingredients that, if mistakenly selected, can ruin your fine work. I well remember watching a good friend turn out a special dinner for me some years back. She was very conscientiously following a "gourmet" recipe as we had a drink and caught up on old news. At the dinner table, after tasting the dish (scallops with a white sauce), she remarked that the sauce didn't taste as good as she had remembered it. What did I think? The answer was simple: The bottled (reconstituted!) lemon juice she had used. Another friend had a disappointing experience using vanillin, a poor imitation of vanilla made from coal tar. Her reason was economy, but when we use so little vanilla anyway and the taste of the artificial product is so inferior, what saving is there? What follows are some thoughts on some of the more frequently used ingredients in this book. Even the best of cooks cannot rise above his or her ingredients!

ARMAGNAC: Simca taught me long ago that this fine brandy from France is almost always best to use in any recipe calling for Cognac or brandy because of its greater depth of flavor. (All Cognacs and Armagnacs are brandies, but not all brandies are Cognacs or Armagnacs.)

BOUQUET GARNI: This is most simply parsley, bay leaf (use half a leaf if it's strong California bay laurel) and thyme (preferably leaf), tied up in cheesecloth for easy removal. Always use fresh parsley, including the stems, which have the most flavor. Do not use those expensive little prepackaged bouquets garnis. If you find it too much trouble to put a bouquet garni in cheesecloth, buy a stainless steel teaball that you can use repeatedly.

BUTTER: Always use sweet, unsalted butter. I know that this can be difficult to find in many parts of the country, but try anyway. If enough people start buying it then more will become available in your area. Salted butter is quite different. Salt not only masks rancidity to a certain degree but also changes the flavor of the butter. (Try comparing sweet butter which you salt yourself with presalted butter.) If unsalted butter is impossible to find, reduce the salt in the recipe.

CHEESE: Cheese as a flavoring ingredient is often underestimated, and the quality is of prime importance. If Gruyère or Swiss is called for, be certain to use a good imported cheese from either France or Switzerland. If Parmesan is called for, obtain at least three-year-old Reggiano imported from Italy, and not the dreadful imitations made in America. Reggiano keeps up to six months, refrigerated in a plastic bag, with a damp paper towel in the bag to keep the cheese from drying out. A very acceptable substitute is American-made Asiago. Asiago is excellent for pasta and, like Parmesan, can be kept, refrigerated, for a good six months.

CHIVES: If you can't find fresh chives, use the green tops of scallions or spring onions cut lengthwise into strips the size of chives, then minced. Do not use "Chinese chives," as the taste is quite different.

CORNICHONS: The French make only this one kind of pickle, a small, very sour variety. This is an excellent accompaniment to the richness of a pâté and is available in jars at most specialty food stores. Sweet American gherkins are not an acceptable substitute.

CREAM CHEESE: The terrible product produced by most large food companies (the only one known to most Americans) can be appreciated only by a taste comparison with fresh cream cheese. The gums and preservatives used give it an acrid flavor which I find wrecks most recipes. If you can't get fresh cream cheese, try to find a good farmer's cheese or use pot cheese with a little salt.

CRÈME FRAÎCHE: It's impossible to approximate this exactly, but if it is not yet available in your area you can make your own in the following way: Warm a cup or more of heavy cream until it is tepid (too much heat will kill the culture), add a tablespoon of yogurt or sour cream and mix well; let stand in an open jar, covered with cheesecloth to keep out dust, in a warm place

(like a turned-off oven) for eight to 24 hours or until thickened. (The mixture will thicken only if it's warm enough and the culture, whether sour cream or yogurt, is still active.) Then place it in the refrigerator overnight, and it will thicken some more. To finish the job properly, "squeeze" it by placing it in a sieve layered with cheesecloth, and refrigerate it overnight to let the whey drip off. This process gets rid of excess water and concentrates the butterfat. The crème fraîche will keep a good 10 days refrigerated and may be used with superior results in almost any recipe calling for either heavy cream or sour cream.

DOUBLE-SMOKED BACON or **HAM:** The extra smoking imparts a special flavor impossible to duplicate. It's worth getting this for recipes that call for it. Schaller & Weber of 1654 Second Avenue, New York, NY 10028, (1-212) 879-3047, can provide it, and of course it can be frozen and stored.

EGGS: Always use "large" or "extra large" eggs. Eggs keep up to six weeks after purchase if they are refrigerated or kept cool. Whipping egg whites is most effective if the eggs are at room temperature.

FLOUR: In this book "flour" refers to *bleached*, all-purpose flour. Flour can spoil, especially whole wheat flour. Flour kept in the refrigerator or freezer will tend to produce a flakier pastry.

LEMON JUICE: Only freshly squeezed juice is acceptable. Don't *ever* use any bottled or frozen varieties, and don't use leftover lemon juice, even if you yourself have squeezed it, because it develops an acrid taste. (However, Clay Triplette taught me that bottled lemon juice is good for freshening up smelly cutting boards.) Lemons keep for a good many weeks when refrigerated, and even cut ones will keep for several days if they are well wrapped.

NUTMEG: Pre-ground nutmeg is acceptable, but freshly ground is best. Like all spices, nutmeg tends to lose strength when it is ground and bottled. A nutmeg grater is inexpensive, and whole nutmegs can usually be found in a health food store that carries food products.

OILS: In France, peanut oil is used frequently for cooking, but it's quite different from the peanut oil sold here. American peanut oil is heavy and viscous, almost as unpleasant as corn oil; French peanut oil is quite light and tasteless. I always use safflower oil, but if you do so, make sure that the brand you choose is light.

When olive oil is called for, use a good French extra-virgin olive oil unless the dish is supposed to have a Mediterranean or Italian flavor. In the latter case a fruity green olive oil, preferably one imported from Sicily, will give the correct taste.

ONIONS: If you want the sweetness that onions can offer (as in the Onion Quiche), select yellow ones; if you want a sharp onion taste, the white ones are preferable.

PARSLEY: Only fresh parsley is acceptable. The touch that parsley adds to a dish is often the taste of freshness. Dried parsley tastes the way it smells, like dried grass. Fresh parsley can keep for up to two weeks if you put it in a large covered jar with a little water in the bottom, just enough to keep the stems moist. Italian or "flat-leaf" parsley has the best flavor; the more common "curly" parsley is prettiest for garnishing; "Chinese" parsley (which is really fresh coriander or cilantro) is not acceptable as a substitute.

SALT: Try to find a brand of salt without sugar added to it (read the label and watch out for dextrose and other words ending in "ose"). Sea salt is preferable for flavor, but kosher salt is good to use as well.

SHALLOTS: These are becoming more widely available. If your vegetable stand doesn't carry them, they are certainly obtainable by mail; addresses are to be found in the small ads in every cooking magazine. Shallots should always be kept on hand, but if you are out of stock you may substitute the white part of scallions or spring onions. You can also use a little onion, cooking it for about five minutes instead of the two minutes it usually takes to cook shallots, or even a pinch of garlic, which takes only about 30 seconds to cook.

VANILLA: Vanillin, a synthetic, is not acceptable; use only true vanilla.

ZEST: The zest of citrus fruit is the colored part of the skin, which carries a lot of oils and most of the taste; the white part of the skin is the pith and is bitter. For zest for a savory dish, grate the fruit over wax paper using the smallest rough portion of the grater; then, using a toothpick, go along the diagonals of the rough front side of the grater to scrape off whatever zest has adhered to it. You can use your fingers to clear the smooth inside of the grater. For a dessert, sometimes a sugar cube is rubbed all over the fruit to pick up the oils, then the sugar cube is included, crushed, in the recipe along with the zest.

Special Equipment

For making quiches and pâtés, there is very little equipment needed that is not usually found in the average kitchen. Any sort of pie pan will do for quiches, and any sort of loaf pan will do for pâtés. But there are a few items that will help immeasurably, and these are described below.

CHEESECLOTH: This is used for many purposes, from "squeezing" homemade crème fraîche to poaching galantines and ballotines. It is difficult to find really good cheesecloth in most stores, so I suggest writing or calling the source I use, which has the finest cheesecloth I've ever seen: The Vermont Country Store, Weston, Vermont 05161, (1-802) 824-6932. Ask for the "Finest Weave Cotton Cheesecloth," order number 13129.

ELECTRIC MIXER: I use a portable hand mixer for small tasks like creaming butter and whipping cream. A blender or food processor will not do as good a job.

FOOD MILL: This very inexpensive "poor man's blender" has some advantages over both the blender and the food processor. Although it is slower, you can control the texture, which can be important. Buy a food mill with three interchangeable discs, not a single permanent one. This is essential for obtaining fine-textured pâtés and is also excellent for making tomato sauce. (Chop whole tomatoes roughly, cook for a few minutes, run through the food mill to remove skin and seeds, return to saucepan and cook to desired consistency.)

FOOD PROCESSOR: This excellent instrument makes it possible to do a host of things that were formerly only within the reach of professionals. It is often used in making pâtés (although a good meat grinder will do a better job) and is excellent for pastry. Buy a brand with a lot of power, because chopping meat is no small task. It is here, and also in grating hard cheeses, that the cheaper food processors will soon give up.

PÂTÉ MOLD or **TERRINE:** Although any ordinary loaf pan will do, if you enjoy making pâtés you'll certainly want to own a nice mold in which you can also serve the pâté at an informal luncheon. Most of the recipes in this book can be made in either a six- or an eight-cup mold. My favorite is a narrow rectangular one made by Le Creuset in enameled cast iron.

QUICHE PAN or **TART MOLD:** Although most quiches can be made in a pie pan (and a pie pan is needed if you are making a quiche with my Fear-of-Pastry Crust), the sloping sides of the typical pie pan will prevent you from being able to unmold the quiche, which always makes for a finer presentation. I suggest buying two or three sizes of the traditional round quiche pans. They have wavy edges, are about one inch high, and have bottoms that can be removed. They come in eight-, nine- and 10-inch sizes.

SPATULAS, SPOONS: Rubber spatulas are my favorite implement for folding—I use a very large one. Wooden spoons should always be used with metal pots; they're heatproof, don't scrape the metal, and may be safely run through the dishwasher. What could be better?

TAMIS: These lovely French instruments are also called drum sieves. They come in various diameters, various materials (nylon or metal) and various degrees of mesh. One of the most useful ones is in stainless steel with interchangeable meshes, available from my favorite supply store, The Bridge Company, 214 East 52nd Street, New York, NY 10022, (1-212) 688-4220. If you buy a tamis with a fixed mesh, I would suggest one of about 30 holes to the inch, size "350." A tamis can be used to improvise a steamer, but its primary purpose is to obtain the fine texture required in certain pâtés and quenelles. In making Smoked Salmon Pâté, it is virtually impossible to get the necessary fine texture without a tamis (but be forewarned, it takes work).

ZESTER: Use the smallest-hole scraping edge of a four-sided grater to remove the outer skin (zest) from citrus fruits.

Basic Techniques and Terminology

ASPIC: An aspic is no more than jelled stock. It is not worth having, making or eating unless it is excellent, because the temperature and the consistency tend to emphasize the smallest defects. It is called for in this book only when making a *pâté en croûte* and, if you wish, with a galantine. Make certain that your stock has excellent flavor and is highly seasoned, because cold cuts the flavor a great deal, more than you'd expect. Chill it well and remove all the fat that solidifies on the top. Strain well and reheat.

Meanwhile, dissolve one package of unflavored gelatin for each two cups of stock (be certain to measure carefully) in a few tablespoons of *cold* stock taken from the measured stock, or in wine, such as Madeira or port, if your recipe calls for flavored aspic. Add the gelatin to the warming stock as well as two or more egg whites, slightly beaten; and add their crushed shells as well, to clarify the stock. Stir slowly but continuously until the stock comes to the boil. Immediately reduce the heat to the barest simmer and cook 10 to 15 minutes. (It is not necessary to stir while the stock is simmering.) Slowly the egg whites will rise to the surface and a dirty crust will form. Turn off the heat and let it rest another 10 minutes.

Place a paper napkin in a strainer as a filter (paper towels, coffee filters and the like will not work as well) and gently ladle the stock with the egg whites into the strainer. Let it drip through slowly. The result should be perfectly crystalline. If it is not, reheat without adding more gelatin and strain once again.

It is always wise to check the jelling quality of the aspic. When placed, at room temperature, in a 40-degree Fahrenheit refrigerator, it should set in 10 to 15 minutes. If it does not, try adding more gelatin in the same manner and test again.

BAIN MARIE: A water bath. The term usually refers to the technique of cooking something in a vessel surrounded with water in an oven or over the heat in a double boiler. In this book the term always refers to a vessel, usually a loaf pan or terrine, sitting in a larger baking dish and surrounded with hot water. The purpose is to distribute the heat evenly as well as to keep it from rising above 212 degrees F., which it cannot do if it is sitting in water, since at that temperature the water turns to steam. When putting the water into the baking dish, make sure that it is boiling. The oven should be preheated.

BLANCH: To cook in water at a rolling boil. If you are blanching vegetables, use as large an amount of salted water as possible, keep testing for doneness ("al dente"—crisp to the bite but certainly cooked), remove immediately and "refresh" in icy cold water to stop the cooking. As soon as the vegetable is at room temperature, remove it from the cold water. If you are blanching almonds, simply place them in a small amount of boiling water (salt is not necessary) for 45 seconds, remove, and when cool enough to touch, rub vigorously in a clean dish towel; most of the skins will slip off. For those that do not, simply pinch the almonds between your thumb and index finger and they'll shoot out of their skins.

CHOP (ONIONS): Cut in half through the root, then cut the tips of the non-root ends off and peel. Carefully cut slices up to *but not through* the root end in one direction, then repeat in a perpendicular direction; finally cut slices across, which will result in even dice, and discard the root end, which has been holding everything together up to this point. A food processor is unsatisfactory for this purpose, because it mashes the onions.

CLARIFY: To clarify stock, see *Aspic*. When clarifying butter, do a fairly large quantity and store it (clarified butter keeps for up to 30 days refrigerated). Melt at least eight ounces (two sticks) of unsalted butter in a saucepan, bring to the simmer and continue cooking about 10 minutes. Do not let it burn. Milk solids on the top will turn slightly brown, milk solids on the bottom will tend to stick there, and the clarified butter in the middle will be crystal clear. Pour it through several thicknesses of good cheesecloth or a cloth coffee filter attached to a short stick, available in most grocery stores. Discard the milk solids.

CREAM: To cream a substance means to bring it to a soft, whipped consistency at which it will easily absorb or be absorbed into another substance. To cream butter, let it come to room temperature, then whip with an electric hand beater until it is the consistency of whipped cream.

FOLD: To combine either whipped egg whites or cream with another substance. Always begin by stirring some of the whipped substance into the heavier substance to lighten it. Then, using a large rubber spatula, scoop up some of the light substance and cut down into the center of the heavier one to the bottom of the bowl, then scrape up the side nearest you; continue cutting down into the center and scraping up the side as you turn the bowl an eighth turn with each cut. Think of folding as "layering," putting layers of the lighter substance into the heavier one. As soon as the lighter substance is fairly evenly incorporated, scoop up some more. Do not overfold—leave some of the white showing—unless the recipe specifically calls for folding until the white disappears. The objective is to keep as much air as possible in the mixture. Overfolding or ordinary mixing will take air out.

GLAZE: The French word *dorer*, "to glaze," means to gild or paint with gold. Pastry is usually glazed twice, once after being formed and then again just before it is put into the oven. You may use an egg yolk (for the darkest color) or a whole egg beaten with a bit of cream or milk or plain water (for the lightest color). Paint the glaze on with a small brush reserved for this purpose.

INFUSE: To give one substance, such as milk or cream, the flavor of another. Usually you boil the two together, then strain: Herbal teas are called "infusions" in French.

JULIENNE: To cut in thin strips, usually from three to five inches in length and about ⅛ inch in width and breadth.

MINCE: To chop finely. Garlic should always be minced with a knife, by hand, unless the recipe calls for crushing or mashing it, which a garlic press does beautifully. To mince garlic, follow the directions for chopping onions, using a small paring knife and omitting the step of cutting it in half through the root, because garlic usually has a flat side. To peel garlic, smack it with a large knife; you often hear a sort of "pop," then the skin peels very easily. Chives should always be cut (minced) in one direction, perpendicular to the way they grow; otherwise they will have a bitter taste.

PEEL (TOMATOES, PEACHES): Drop the fruit in boiling water for 15 seconds, remove and break the skin with the tip of a sharp knife; the skins should come off easily. If they don't, the fruit is not really ripe enough. But if you put it back into the boiling water for another 30 seconds, the skins will probably come off.

PRESERVE, HOLD (PÂTÉS): All pâtés baked in loaf pans can be preserved for two to three months by sealing them with rendered fat (melted leaf lard will do nicely) and refrigerating them—but they *must* be *thoroughly* sealed. Freezing is unsatisfactory.

RENDER (FAT): Rendering fat is somewhat akin to clarifying butter. Fat is composed of a solid substance and the part that melts down; think of the solid part as rather like the milk solids that remain in the pan when clarifying butter. To render chicken fat, simply cover it with water and bring to the boil, then simmer about 15 minutes until you hear a crackling or splattering sound. When this subsides, the fat is rendered. There should be no trace of water, only a clear, golden liquid. Strain out the solid parts (they can be fried and eaten) and chill the liquid as you would clarified butter. To render the fat of pork or beef, first chop it (a meat grinder is best) and let it soak overnight in cold water; then render it in a baking pan in the oven. It goes through the same steps as chicken fat but is a bit harder to work with. Freshly rendered pork fat, not to be confused with the processed and preserved lard one buys in a store, gives excellent flavor to pastry.

RIBBON: Whenever you beat eggs with sugar, you are "ribboning." The purpose is to distribute the egg evenly and also to keep the mixture from becoming granular. Never combine the sugar and eggs ahead of time and let them sit; the sugar will begin to "cook" the eggs, causing a chemical change. In ribboning the mixture will be orange-ish at first, then it will begin to lighten and become a pale yellow, which is what you are looking for. If you lift the turned-off beater, the mixture should slowly run down and fall into the bowl, looking just like a yellow ribbon. (If you try this earlier when you are just beginning to combine the eggs and sugar, you will note a marked difference.)

SAUTÉ: This means to cook in a pan *lubricated* with fat. It differs from frying, which technically means cooking something *immersed* in fat.

SEED: Cucumbers are seeded to remove the slight bitterness that the seeds impart. Cut the cucumbers in half lengthwise, then simply scoop out the seeds by scraping down with a teaspoon.

SPLAY (CORNICHONS or SMALL PICKLES): Splaying is a decorative technique and is quite attractive. Make several cuts up to but not through the stem end of the pickle, which will spread slightly, like a little fan. Cornichons are usually presented this way on a platter with slices of pâté.

STOCK: To make a stock, take the bones of whatever meat you are using and proceed in one of two ways: For a brown stock you must sear the bones, meat and vegetables (the basics are a sliced carrot, a sliced stalk of celery and a sliced onion, without the skin, together with a bouquet garni). For a white stock this step is omitted.

Searing may be done by sautéing or by roasting in an oven until well browned. Classicists then put the bones, meat and vegetables in a large pot; cover with a good quantity of *unsalted* cold water, bring to the boil, and simmer for several hours while skimming the scum that rises to the top. I prefer to hold back the vegetables and furiously boil the bones and meat alone until there is a nice flavor (high heat is more efficient for getting minerals out of bones, but it wrecks vegetables). At the very end I turn off the heat and add diced vegetables for 15 minutes, which is enough time to get out all of their nutrients. I do not skim—the scum is a protein that is good for you. If I want the stock clear, it is easy to clarify it afterward (see *Aspic*). Cook the stock until there is good flavor. If the water gets too low, add more.

The more bones and meat you have, the better. I save the carcasses from roasted chicken in the freezer until I have enough for a good stock. Many other ingredients may be added to a stock: some white wine as part of the liquid, additional vegetables such as garlic and tomatoes, etc. For more on stocks, consult a good French cookbook, such as *Mastering the Art of French Cooking* by Simone Beck and Julia Child.

WATER BATH: See *Bain Marie.*

WHIPPING CREAM: It is best to use real cream, not ultra-pasteurized, if at all possible. *Everything* should be icy cold: the cream, the bowl, the beaters. If the bowl is not well chilled, place it in a larger bowl filled with ice cubes and cold water. Begin whipping the cream slowly and gradually increase the speed. Cream goes through two stages: the *crème chantilly* or soft-peak stage, and the stiff-peak stage. At the soft-peak stage, which most recipes require, when the turned-off beater is lifted straight up, a peak is left in the bowl, but when the bowl is tilted the peak will flow or move. At the stiff-peak stage, the same peak will not move when the bowl is tilted. The primary use of stiffly beaten cream is for decorating; softly beaten cream is best for mousses. Do not beat cream beyond the stiff-peak stage or it may turn into butter. If this happens, drain it in cheesecloth, squeeze, refrigerate and use it as butter. Cream on the verge of turning sour can quickly be made into butter.

WHIPPING EGG WHITES: This requires the opposite conditions to whipping cream—older egg whites are preferred, at room temperature. A copper bowl (always clean it, just before using it, with a tablespoon of salt and a tablespoon of white distilled vinegar or lemon juice, rubbing well, rinsing with hot water and drying with a paper towel) and a large balloon whisk are best, or a copper bowl and an electric hand mixer moved around a lot. Stainless steel bowls are also satisfactory, but not plastic or glass.

Begin beating slowly to break up the egg whites, then add a pinch of salt (plus a pinch of cream of tartar if you are *not* using a copper bowl, to compensate for the acid from the copper). Keep beating in large sweeps to move the entire mass of egg whites. There are two stages, soft and hard peaks. Test for soft peaks by lifting the whisk *straight up* from the middle of the bowl and turning it whisk-end up. The egg whites will begin to droop, indicating soft peaks (if they fall rather than droop slowly, they're not yet at the soft-peak stage). Unless you are using them at this stage (which is when it's best to begin adding sugar, if called for), continue beating but stop and test frequently. When the peaks stand up stiffly, they are ready. Use immediately; if you must hold them, cover with plastic wrap but don't expect them to stand up for long.

About Short Pastry

The pastry used for quiches is remarkably similar to that used for pâtes, both being variations of short pastry, or pâte brisée. Both quiches and pâtés may be made without pastry, in which case quiches are then called flans or gratins, and pâtés become terrines, galantines or ballotines. If you have a fear of pastry, start out the easy way, with no crust—or use the Fear-of-Pastry Crust (page 31) for quiches until you get the confidence to try the real thing.

Pâte brisée is the most useful all-purpose dough in French cooking. With sugar added it becomes *pâte sucrée* (sweet short pastry); with sugar and eggs it becomes *pâte sablée* (meaning "sandy pastry" because of its texture); and with a minimal amount of butter or fat and a little extra salt it becomes *pâte à pâté* (pâté dough).

As you have probably read or been told many times, pastry-making is an exact science, as cooking is not. A little more of this or less of that in making a quiche filling or a forcemeat for a pâté probably won't hurt anything. But changing the type of flour, using baking powder that's too old or improperly measuring or weighing some ingredient can turn your pastry into a disaster. In the pastry recipes that follow, measurements are given by weight (in grams and ounces) and by volume.

At its very finest pâte brisée is a mixture, *by weight*, of five parts flour to four parts butter (the weight of the butter equals 80 percent of the weight of the flour); or for the pastry generally used to line a pâté mold, the butter may be reduced to only 20 percent the weight of the flour. A small amount of salt is added, plus enough cold water to "make a dough."

An important component of wheat flour is gluten, some flours having more than others. When gluten is wet, it binds together to form an invisible elastic web. If you simply mixed water with flour, the resulting pastry would be hard and tough, like the crust on a loaf of good bread. However, if fat coats some of the gluten particles, preventing moisture from letting them bind, the resulting pastry is flaky and crisp. This is why we add butter—but don't let it melt or get soft or it won't coat the gluten particles.

The more water in your dough and the more handling (or kneading) you do, the tougher and harder your pastry will be. Kneading also develops the elasticity in a dough, which is desirable in bread but not in pastry. The more fat and the less water you add, the more crumbly, fragile and cookie-like the dough becomes.

When working with pâte brisée, a big challenge is to avoid shrinkage and obtain light, flaky pastry. The main rule is not to rush things; in fact, if you plan to bake quiches, it's best to make your pastry a day in advance and refrigerate it. The gluten in the dough relaxes with time and coldness, making for lighter pastry. If you must make a dough in a hurry, use egg as your primary liquid. The dough will be fragile and crisp, will shrink much less than a dough made without egg, and need not be refrigerated. I always make twice as much pastry as I need, freezing what I don't use, so that I always have some ready with an hour's notice for defrosting.

Another problem with quiche pastry is what I call soggy bottoms—doughy or wet pastry. There are many ways of dealing with this, but the simplest I've found is to prebake all quiche shells fully. You might expect that baking a filling for 30 minutes or more in a fully baked shell would overbake the pastry, but it does not.

A good solution to the problem of overworking the dough (characteristic of beginners) is to use a food processor. Although I agree fundamentally with the French maxim, "Il faut mettre la main à la pâte" (You must get your hands in the dough), this is not a pastry book, so all the recipes are made with a food processor. If you wish to do them by hand I recommend the excellent directions in *Mastering the Art of French Cooking*.

General Tips for Making Short Pastry

Flour
For a flaky dough, keep your flour very cold, even in the freezer.

If you intend to be a serious cook or baker, measure by weight. Only amateurs work with the imprecision of volume measurement. If you have no scale, then scoop with a dry-measure cup (not a glass one) and sweep off the excess with the straight edge of a knife.

Always sift the flour to aerate it, even if a recipe doesn't call for sifting. Use a sieve; flour sifters are a nuisance to keep clean and don't do the job any more effectively than an ordinary sieve.

Replacing one quarter to one third of the butter with shortening or lard will result in a flakier pastry. (I don't do this because of the preservatives and chemical processing in shortenings and most lard.)

Use flour with a low gluten percentage—look for the protein percentage on the package. Fifteen percent is high and will result in more shrinkage than a flour with, say, 11 percent.

Rolling Out
Make certain that your dough has been refrigerated long enough, at best two hours. But don't let it get too cold or the butter won't give and you'll have trouble rolling it. If this happens, let it sit at room temperature for five to 10 minutes before rolling out.

Work quickly—if it takes more than two minutes to roll out, you're overworking the dough.

If you want to roll a very thin sheet of dough, don't make a big ball when refrigerating it; form a thinnish disc. If the dough is already in a big ball, cut it in half horizontally.

Roll gently outward in all directions, trying not to push down. There's no truth to the maxim that you should only roll away from yourself—watch professional bakers if you don't believe me.

If the dough retracts very much when being rolled, it needs more refrigeration to relax the gluten.

Turn the dough after each roll. Quarter turns will result in a square sheet of dough, eighth turns will result in a round sheet.

If the dough sticks when you are rolling out, sprinkle a bit of flour on the board and on the dough. Try not to add too much flour or the dough will get tougher.

Finally, let it rest, rolled out, for five to 10 minutes before cutting it.

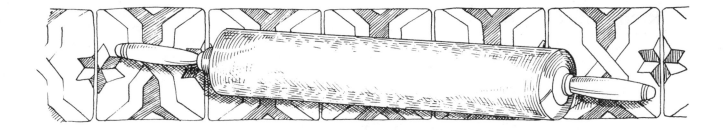

Ordinary Short Pastry *(Pâte Brisée)*

8- to 10-inch quiche shell

This pastry will work for all the quiches, both savory and sweet. There is no egg in the dough, so it needs the full resting time in order to avoid shrinkage. It has a fine flavor and, when made properly, will be crisp and flaky.

Cold flour	250 grams	8 ounces	1¾ cups
Salt	5 grams	1 teaspoon	1 teaspoon
Cold butter, diced	125 grams	4 ounces	8 tablespoons
Ice water	1 deciliter	4 ounces	½ cup

NOTE: *Use one column of measurements; do not switch to another for other ingredients, as the columns are not exact equivalents.*

Place the cold flour in the bowl of a food processor fitted with a steel cutting blade. Add the salt and process by turning the processor on and off once.

Add the butter to the bowl. Turn the processor on and off 4 to 5 times, until the butter is cut into the flour in about the size of lima beans—not too small.

With the processor running, add the ice water and process for approximately 5 seconds. *Do not wait until the dough forms a ball before turning off the processor.* Remove the dough from the bowl and put it in a plastic bag. Quickly press it together into a disc (ready for rolling out) and refrigerate for at least 2 hours. Do not seal the bag tightly; let the dough breathe a bit.

Rich Short Pastry

This pastry, like the preceding one, will work for all the quiches, savory and sweet. It uses the maximum amount of butter and an egg for an even richer taste.

Cold flour	250 grams	8 ounces	1¾ cups
Salt	5 grams	1 teaspoon	1 teaspoon
Cold butter, diced	180 grams	6 ounces	12 tablespoons
Egg	1 large	1 large	1 large
Ice water	¾ deciliter	⅓ cup	5½ tablespoons

NOTE: *Use one column of measurements; do not switch to another for other ingredients, as the columns are not exact equivalents.*

Place the cold flour in the bowl of a food processor fitted with a steel cutting blade. Add the salt and turn the processor on and off once.

Add the butter to the bowl. Turn the processor on and off 4 to 5 times. The butter should be cut into the flour in about the size of lima beans—not too small.

Mix the egg and water together. With the processor running, add the mixture and process for approximately 5 seconds. *Do not wait until the dough forms a ball before turning off the processor.* Remove the dough from the bowl and put it in a plastic bag. Quickly press it together into a disc (ready for rolling out) and refrigerate for at least 2 hours. Do not seal the bag tightly.

Sweet Short Pastry *(Pâte Sucrée)*

This pastry uses the maximum amount of both butter and sugar, so it is basically for dessert quiches and tarts. For a slightly better flavor include a whole egg or an egg yolk as part of the liquid (measure the liquid in a container that already has the egg in it). Extra-fine sugar is best. Confectioners' (powdered) sugar may also be used, but in this case be certain to measure by weight (columns 1 or 2) or, if working by volume, to use twice the amount of sugar that is given below.

Cold flour	250 grams	8 ounces	1¾ cups
Salt	Pinch	Pinch	Pinch
Sugar	75 grams	2½ ounces	⅓ cup
Cold butter, diced	200 grams	6½ ounces	12 tablespoons
Ice water	¾ deciliter	⅓ cup	5½ tablespoons
Vanilla (optional)	1 teaspoon	1 teaspoon	1 teaspoon

NOTE: *Use one column of measurements; do not switch to another for other ingredients, as the columns are not exact equivalents.*

Place the cold flour in the bowl of a food processor fitted with a steel cutting blade. Add the salt and sugar and turn the processor on and off once.

Add the butter to the bowl. Turn the processor on and off 4 to 5 times. The butter should be cut into the flour in the size of lima beans—not too small.

Mix the ice water with the egg and vanilla if you choose to use them. (The total volume of these liquids should not exceed the quantity listed for water.) With the processor running add the mixture or the water alone and process for approximately 5 seconds. *Do not wait until the dough forms a ball before turning off the processor.* Remove the dough from the bowl and put it in a plastic bag, quickly press it together into a disc (ready for rolling out) and refrigerate it for at least 2 hours. Do not seal the bag tightly.

NOTE. This dough will be rather crumbly and can be difficult to roll out. Be certain that it warms up a bit before you roll it out. It should feel cool but not cold.

Rich Almond-Egg Short Pastry (*Pâte Sablée*) *8- to 10-inch quiche shell*

In France pâte sablée is made without water, but because American flours are drier, water is needed to get the gluten to develop enough to hold the dough together when it is rolled out. Pâte sablée (sandy pastry) need be no more than a short pastry with sugar and egg, but it is a current vogue to add pulverized almonds, which gives the pastry a delicious flavor and makes it even "sandier." Extra-fine sugar is best. Confectioners' (powdered) sugar may also be used, but in this case go by weight, or if working by volume use twice the amount of sugar that is given below.

Cold flour	250 grams	8 ounces	1¾ cups
Salt	Pinch	Pinch	Pinch
Sugar	60 grams	2 ounces	¼ cup
Pulverized almonds	60 grams	2 ounces	½ cup
Cold butter, diced	180 grams	6 ounces	12 tablespoons
Egg	1 large	1 large	1 large
Ice water	1 deciliter	2 tablespoons	2 tablespoons
Vanilla	½ teaspoon	½ teaspoon	½ teaspoon

NOTE: *Use one column of measurements; do not switch to another for other ingredients, as the columns are not exact equivalents.*

Place the cold flour in the bowl of a food processor fitted with a steel cutting blade. Add the salt, sugar and almonds, and turn the processor on and off once.

Add the butter to the bowl. Turn the processor on and off 4 to 5 times. The butter should be cut into the flour in the size of lima beans.

Mix the egg, ice water and vanilla together. With the processor running, add the mixture and process for approximately 5 seconds. *Do not wait until the dough forms a ball before turning off the processor.* Remove the dough from the bowl and put it in a plastic bag. Quickly press it together into a disc (ready for rolling out) and refrigerate for at least 2 hours. Do not seal the bag tightly.

Quiche

About Quiches

Quiche, or kiche (this spelling you sometimes see in France) reputedly originated in the Lorraine area. There are several types of quiches in France. Each region of Lorraine and Alsace has its own and of course feels *that* is the true quiche.

A quiche is simply a custard plus morsels of meat, fish, poultry or vegetables and/or grated cheese baked in a tart shell, usually made of short pastry. The same mixture may also be baked without a crust in a buttered baking dish, thereby becoming a gratin.

Simple rules for making a quiche filling:

1. The custard mixture is generally based on the proportion of a whole large egg per ¾ cup of cream or milk.

2. Precooked food should go into the shell before the custard filling. Grated cheese and flavorings are usually mixed into the custard.

3. A quiche shell should be no more than about three-quarters full before it is baked, to allow for rising. An 8-inch shell will take about 2½ cups of filling, a 10-inch shell about 3¾ cups.

4. Cooking times are generally 30 minutes in a 375-degree oven, 60 minutes in a 250-degree oven. The quiche is done when a knife stuck into the center comes out clean.

5. Savory quiches usually contain seasonings such as salt, pepper, nutmeg, cayenne, allspice and saffron. Sweet quiches usually contain 2 tablespoons of sugar per cup of custard.

Lining Quiche Molds

After rolling out the dough to a ⅛-inch thickness, let it rest 5 to 10 minutes. Gently roll the dough up on the rolling pin. Then, sloppily, letting it overlap everywhere, unroll it over the mold.

Lift the extremities up and let the dough fill the corners of the mold, using a little ball of extra dough to push it gently into the corners.

With scissors, trim the dough about ¾ inch beyond the edge of the mold, then turn this extra part over and down on the inside to form a thicker edge (about ¼ inch) all around.

With your thumbs, gently press the dough up about ¼ inch above the top rim of the mold.

With the dull edge of a small knife, gently score the dough coming up over the mold's rim at 1-inch intervals. This helps to keep the pastry from shrinking and decorates the edge.

Prick the quiche shell all over with the tines of a fork. The tiny holes allow steam to escape and help keep the center from bubbling up.

After lining the mold and pricking the shell, place it in the freezer for 30 minutes to 1 hour. It is even better if baked frozen.

Baking Quiche Shells

Preheat the oven and a baking sheet to 400 degrees. (Putting the mold onto a preheated baking sheet helps to obtain a drier and flakier crust.)

Cover the quiche shell with aluminum foil, then fill it with dried beans, chickpeas, clean pebbles or little aluminum pellets. Place the mold on the baking sheet in the middle of the oven for 8 to 9 minutes.

Take the quiche shell out of the oven, shutting the door immediately. Remove the aluminum foil and beans, prick again with a fork all over, then return to the oven for another 8 to 9 minutes.

Remove the shell from the oven, paint the bottom with a beaten whole egg or egg white, or Dijon-style mustard if you are making a savory quiche, or strained apricot or currant jam if it is a sweet quiche. Return it to the oven and leave until fully baked, usually another 4 to 6 minutes.

When the shell is fully baked, unmold it and slip it onto a rack to dry out the bottom.

NOTE: If the shell has cracked, do not remove it from the mold.

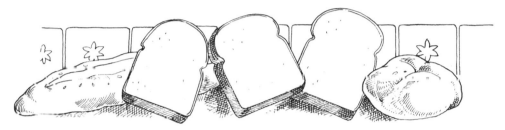

Fear-of-Pastry Crust

8- to 10-inch quiche shell

I got this idea from Simone Beck when I was experimenting with the recipe for two-cheese flan from her book New Menus from Simca's Cuisine. *I found that the flan almost had a crust, and once I even unmolded and reversed the flan with complete success. So if you are in a hurry or are reluctant to try pastry dough, or if you just want to cut back on the amount of calories you're consuming and serving, this simple "crust" will do the trick. For a dessert quiche, substitute cookie crumbs for the breadcrumbs.*

3-4 tablespoons unsalted butter, at room temperature
8-12 tablespoons freshly made breadcrumbs

Smear the butter with your fingers very generously all around the bottom and sides of an 8-, 9- or 10-inch pie or cake pan with a fixed bottom, or any baking dish suitable for presentation. If the butter is very soft, refrigerate for a few minutes before adding the breadcrumbs.

Sprinkle all the breadcrumbs over the butter and tilt the dish so that all the buttered surfaces are covered with crumbs. Press the crumbs into the butter with a fork, then knock out any excess by tapping the dish upside down. Refrigerate until ready to use.

NOTE: Breadcrumbs can be made easily with your food processor from stale bread. If the breadcrumbs are too moist and absorbent, dry them out a bit in a 350-degree oven, being careful not to burn them. If you are using fresh bread, put the slices whole into the oven before processing.

Savory Quiches

Quiche Lorraine

Serves 4-6

The original Quiche Lorraine seems to have been a piece of bread dough, much like a pizza crust, smeared with thick cream and eggs, and baked quickly in a hot oven. Today Quiche Lorraine includes eggs, butter, bacon and heavy cream or thick crème fraîche. Nontraditionalists add cheese although it really has no place in a true quiche. The crème fraîche makes it "cheesy" enough. If you can't get crème fraîche you can make your own (see page 15) or use heavy cream. If you cannot obtain double-smoked bacon, use smoked bacon and omit the blanching step.

**8-inch prebaked quiche shell
(see pages 25 and 26)
4 ounces double-smoked bacon
3 large eggs
1½ cups crème fraîche, or
heavy cream
½ teaspoon salt
¼ teaspoon freshly ground pepper
3 tablespoons unsalted butter,
chilled and diced**

Preheat the oven to 375 degrees.

Cut the bacon into little strips and put it into a saucepan of cold water. Heat just to boiling and simmer for 2 minutes. Remove the bacon, drain, and place it in a frying pan. Sauté long enough to render the fat but not long enough for the bacon to become stiff and dry.

Beat the eggs with the cream. Add salt and pepper.

Place the bacon—with some of the drippings too, if you wish—on the bottom of the shell, fill with the egg-cream mixture, dot with chilled butter and bake 25 to 35 minutes, or until the filling is browned and set.

Cheese Quiche

A regular Cheese Quiche, not to be confused with a Quiche Lorraine, is the simplest one of all.

8-inch prebaked quiche shell
  (see pages 25 and 26)
3 large eggs
1½ cups crème fraîche or heavy
  cream
4 ounces freshly grated Gruyère
  cheese
½ teaspoon salt
Freshly ground pepper to taste
3 tablespoons unsalted butter,
  chilled and diced

Preheat the oven to 375 degrees.

Beat the eggs, cream, cheese, salt and pepper together, pour into the quiche shell, dot with the butter and bake 25 to 35 minutes, or until browned and set.

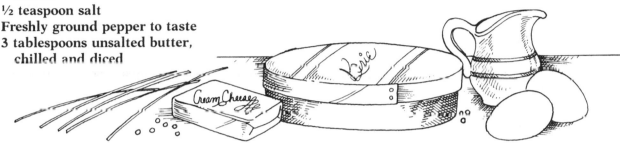

Parisian Brie Quiche

This subtle cheese quiche is an excellent way to begin a dinner, one that your cheese-loving friends will savor and a nice change from the expected.

Select a very ripe Brie, as its strength will be diminished by baking. Any other soft cheese may be substituted, such as a good Reblochon, Camembert, or goat cheese (the popular "Bucheron" is excellent). Be sure to use fresh cream cheese, not one of the gummy commercial brands. Read the label: if any gums or preservatives have been added, don't buy it. If fresh cream cheese is unavailable, use a very mild cottage cheese, ricotta or farmer's cheese.

8-inch prebaked quiche shell
  (see pages 25 and 26)
4 ounces Brie, rind removed
5 ounces fresh cream cheese
2 tablespoons butter, at room
  temperature
3 tablespoons heavy cream
2 large eggs
1 tablespoon minced fresh chives
1 teaspoon salt
Freshly ground pepper

Preheat the oven to 375 degrees.

Cream the cheeses with the butter in an electric mixer or in a food processor. Add the cream, eggs and chives to the cheeses and butter and mix well.

Taste for seasoning and add salt and pepper to taste. Mix well. Pour the mixture into the shell and bake for 25 to 35 minutes, or until browned and set. Let cool 5 minutes before serving.

Eggplant and Yogurt Quiche

Most eggplant dishes from the Western world combine this delectable vegetable with tomatoes, garlic and onions. People in the Middle East combine eggplant with yogurt, lemon and mint for a very special flavor.

Make certain your eggplants are firm and unblemished. Choose a tangy whole-milk yogurt and a good, fruity olive oil, one that smells and tastes of the fruit and has a greenish cast.

**9-inch prebaked quiche shell
(see pages 25 and 26)
2 medium-size eggplants, or
approximately 2 pounds
1 cup plain yogurt
3 large eggs
3 tablespoons olive oil
½ medium-size onion, minced
2 tablespoons minced fresh mint
1½ teaspoons salt
Freshly ground pepper
1 tablespoon lemon juice, freshly
squeezed**

Preheat the oven to 375 degrees.

Cut several slashes in the eggplants and place in the oven for about 50 minutes, until the skins darken and will peel easily.

Remove the pulp from the eggplants and puree it in a food processor. Measure 2 cups of the puree and place in a bowl.

Mix the yogurt with the eggs, olive oil, onion and mint. Add the 2 cups of eggplant puree and season with salt, pepper and lemon juice. Pour into the quiche shell and bake 25 to 35 minutes, or until puffed and set.

NOTE: Any remaining eggplant can be mixed with a bit of yogurt (start with 1 tablespoon) plus the same amount of olive oil and some salt, pepper, and lemon juice. Use as a dip.

Madeira and Ham Quiche

The French have a way of taking an ordinary dish and making something special out of it. This quiche borrows from the classic Quiche Lorraine but increases the amount of ham to make it heartier and gives it a subtle seasoning of Madeira wine, which marries exceptionally well with both ham and cream, not to mention the cheese. For the best flavor, seek out a central European butcher and get some "double-smoked" ham. Use a good cheese—Emmenthaler will also do nicely—and avoid supermarket imitations. A bottle of Madeira is not expensive and should last a long time, but port will do almost as well.

**8-inch prebaked quiche shell
(see pages 25 and 26)
8 ounces smoked ham in ¼-inch
slices with some fat
¼ cup Madeira or port
1 cup heavy cream
2 large eggs
Freshly ground pepper
3-4 ounces Gruyère cheese, freshly
grated**

Preheat the oven to 375 degrees.

Cut the slices of ham into ¼-inch dice, saving all the fat. Cook the fat until rendered in a sauté pan over medium heat. It will release liquid and the solid parts will start to brown. Do not let them burn. Remove and discard the solid particles (or eat them, as I do). Add the ham to the pan and sauté in the fat 3 to 4 minutes, until it begins to brown. Add the wine and cook another 2 to 3 minutes to reduce it.

Mix the cream with the eggs in a bowl, add the ham and Madeira mixture, pepper to taste, and half the cheese. Taste

for seasoning. Pour into the quiche shell and bake for 25 to 35 minutes, or until browned and set.

Sprinkle the top with the remaining cheese and return to the oven until it is melted or run the quiche briefly under the broiler to brown the top.

Minted Spinach Quiche

Serves 4-6

Spinach is a marvelous vegetable which adapts itself to many different unions, with nutmeg, Madeira and cheese, to name only a few of its partners. My son Christopher, who spent some time cooking for a French family, discovered how well mint complements spinach while he was looking for a new way to prepare it that would please some spinach haters in the family. Mint did it. The combination is innovative and exciting, a boon for jaded palates.

The two requisites are simply good spinach, preferably fresh (but a good brand of frozen leaf spinach will do well), and fresh mint. If you can't get fresh mint, wait until you can rather than substitute for it. Sour cream may be substituted for the crème fraîche, but in that case don't attempt to whip it. If you use crème fraîche, don't overwhip it or it may turn to butter.

8-inch prebaked quiche shell
  (see pages 25 and 26)
6 tablespoons unsalted butter
1 pound fresh spinach or 10-ounce
  package frozen leaf spinach,
  defrosted and well drained
2 tablespoons minced fresh mint
1 teaspoon salt
Freshly ground pepper
2 large eggs
1 cup heavy cream
Unsweetened crème fraîche or sour
  cream (optional)

Preheat the oven to 375 degrees.

Dice 2 tablespoons of the butter and refrigerate.

If using fresh spinach (always preferable), blanch it in boiling salted water for 3 minutes, remove, drain, squeeze it dry and chop coarsely.

Melt the remaining butter in a sauté pan, sauté the mint about 30 seconds, add the chopped spinach and stir briefly. Season to taste with salt and pepper.

Mix the eggs with the cream, add the spinach and pour into the quiche shell. Dot with the cold diced butter and bake in the oven 25 to 35 minutes, or until puffed and set.

Serve with a dollop of crème fraîche, briefly whipped, or sour cream, if you like.

Liptauer Quiche

In Austria, where my family has a home in the Alps to which I retreat at least once a year and always when writing, perhaps the most popular cocktail hors d'oeuvre is Liptauer cheese. It is made by hanging thickened milk or cream in several layers of cheesecloth so that the whey or water drips away, thus increasing the density and butterfat. The cheese is then seasoned in a manner typical of Austria, with paprika, onions, chives (the Austrians' favorite herb), caraway seeds and mustard. Having been asked to make some by visiting friends, I wondered what it would be like as a quiche. I think it captures the special tastes of Austria quite admirably.

Cottage cheese may certainly be used here, especially if you can find a nice acidic one. If using cream cheese, use one without gums or preservatives, or substitute farmer's cheese. When mincing chives always cut them in one direction, horizontal to the chives standing up, in order to avoid a bitter taste. Chop the onions by hand (see page 20)—a food processor will mash them.

**8-inch prebaked quiche shell
 (see pages 25 and 26)**
6 tablespoons unsalted butter
**8 ounces fresh cream cheese, cottage
 cheese or farmer's cheese**
½ cup heavy cream
3 large eggs
2 tablespoons paprika
1 teaspoon salt
1 teaspoon caraway seeds
1½ teaspoons dry mustard
1½ tablespoons capers, minced
4 tablespoons finely chopped onions
4 tablespoons minced chives

Preheat the oven to 375 degrees.

Take half the butter, cut it into dice and refrigerate.

With an electric mixer or in a food processor, cream the cheese, cream, remaining butter and eggs. Stir in all the rest of the ingredients, reserving 1 tablespoon of minced chives.

Pour the mixture into the quiche shell, dot with the refrigerated butter dice and place in the oven to bake for 25 to 35 minutes, or until puffed and brown.

Serve sprinkled with the reserved chives.

Kren Quiche *(Beef with Horseradish)*

Kren is the Austrian word for horseradish, an unusual but delicious ingredient for a quiche that I created to please the palate of a dear friend, Chris-Paul Stapels, the extremely talented Dutch photographer.

Fresh horseradish, if you can find it, is far superior to the bottled variety. It is a root that looks like a long, pale carrot, but be warned: It's addictive! I well remember a student in one of my Austrian cooking classes who became so enraptured with fresh horseradish that she used to grate it over everything except dessert. Fresh horseradish freezes well—simply wrap the root and put it in the freezer. This is definitely a quiche for those who love horseradish, although its strength will be diminished somewhat by the cream.

If you don't have leftover roast beef or a convenient delicatessen that can provide you with slices, buy a small steak and sear it over very high heat in a seasoned iron frying pan, about one minute on each side. Only a little coarse salt sprinkled on the pan itself will be necessary, no fat or oil. The rarer the beef the better, as it will cook more when the quiche is baked.

**9-inch prebaked quiche shell
(see pages 25 and 26)**
**1½-2 cups cooked beef in julienne
strips about ⅛ inch by ⅛ inch and
1-2 inches long**
**1½ cups crème fraîche or heavy
cream**
3 large eggs
**6 ounces bottled horseradish, or the
same amount of fresh horseradish,
peeled and coarsely grated**
1 teaspoon salt
Freshly ground pepper
2 tablespoons freshly minced parsley

Preheat the oven to 375 degrees.

Place the beef strips in the quiche shell, covering the bottom.

In a bowl, mix the cream, eggs, horseradish (with the juices from the bottle if you are not using the fresh root), salt and pepper, and parsley. Pour the horseradish-cream mixture into the quiche shell and bake for 25 to 30 minutes, or until set and beginning to brown.

Mexican Avocado and Cheese Quiche

Serves 4-6

No one is able to recreate the sensual tastes of Mexico better than Diana Kennedy—even the Mexican government has requested her assistance in planning banquets, in addition to recognizing her skill with its highest honors. Her simple and honest guacamole is a proper introduction to her cooking. This quiche begins with some of her ideas but reflects them from a French viewpoint.

Make certain that your avocadoes are good ones and properly ripe. If they are not soft let them sit for a couple of days in a paper bag, not tightly closed. Farmer's cheese replaces the traditional cream in this quiche. It is somewhat similar to Mexico's queso blanco which you should use if you can get it; it gives a more regional taste. The tomatoes should be very ripe and flavorful. Add a chili pepper if you like it hot; for most people Tabasco does a good enough job in a quiche. Fresh coriander is a very special herb which I adore and which is an integral part of Diana's guacamole, but some people do not like it. If you don't share this taste, you'll find the quiche is quite good without it.

9-inch prebaked quiche shell (see pages 25 and 26)
2 cloves garlic, minced
2 ripe avocadoes
1 medium-size white onion, finely chopped
2 ripe medium-size tomatoes
1 cup (8 ounces) queso blanco or farmer's cheese
2 large eggs
1½ teaspoons Tabasco or a small chili pepper, veined, seeded and minced
1 tablespoon minced fresh parsley
1½ teaspoons salt
1 tablespoon minced fresh coriander leaves (optional)

Preheat the oven to 375 degrees.

Mince the garlic by hand as a press will mash it.

Scoop out the pulp of both avocadoes and mash them in a bowl with the garlic and onion.

Cut the tomatoes in half horizontally, squeeze out the water and excess seeds (save this and drink it as a wonderfully fresh tomato juice), then chop them coarsely. Add the tomatoes to the bowl.

With an electric mixer or in a food processor break up the cheese and cream it with the eggs, Tabasco or chili pepper, parsley, salt and coriander, if you wish. By hand, stir in the avocado mixture, pour into the quiche shell and bake 25 to 35 minutes, or until puffed and golden brown on top. This quiche is also good at room temperature, ideal for taking along on picnics.

NOTE: Coriander leaves should not be confused with coriander seeds. It's the same plant but quite a different taste. Fresh coriander is also called cilantro in Spanish markets and Chinese parsley in Oriental markets.

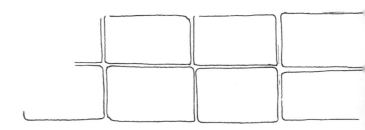

Red and Green Pepper Quiche

Serves 4-6

This colorful quiche has obvious roots in the wonderful cooking of Diana Kennedy. If you still think Mexican cooking is greasy tacos and indigestion you're in for a pleasant discovery when you read and cook from her books. Recently I spent a wonderful week at her home outside Mexico City exploring exciting new dishes and tastes. The remembrance of that led me to develop this "Quiche for Diana."

The technique for peeling peppers is one I learned from Diana. If you don't have a gas stove, then hold the peppers under the broiler. The recipe can of course be made with only green peppers or only red peppers. If you can find yellow peppers, use all three and call this "Three-Pepper Quiche."

**9-inch prebaked quiche shell
(see pages 25 and 26)
4 green peppers
4 red peppers
Small green chili pepper (optional)
3 tablespoons unsalted butter
1 teaspoon salt
Freshly ground black pepper
3 large eggs
¾ cup milk
¾ cup heavy cream
4 ounces Gruyère cheese, freshly
grated**

Preheat the oven to 375 degrees.

Toast the peppers by putting them directly into a gas flame until they are black and blistered on all sides. It will take several minutes altogether. As soon as they are thoroughly blistered all over, place them in a plastic bag for a few minutes.

If you are using the optional chili pepper, carefully cut it in small julienne strips, discarding the seeds and any "ribs." Then mince it very finely. Wash your hands to remove any hot chili oils. (If you wear contact lenses it's best to do this wearing rubber gloves, as the oils can remain on your fingers through many washings.)

After 10 minutes or more remove the peppers from the plastic bag and, putting them under cold running water, pull off the blistered outer skin. Discard the cores and seeds, then cut the peppers into julienne strips about ⅛ inch thick.

Sauté the pepper strips and optional chili pepper in the butter over medium heat 2 to 3 minutes until the butter is absorbed. Add salt and pepper to taste.

Beat the eggs with the milk and cream in a bowl, stir in the pepper mixture and stir again. Sprinkle the cheese on the *bottom* of the quiche shell, pour the pepper mixture over it and bake for 25 to 35 minutes, or until set.

Golden Onion Quiche

I always passed over this quiche (which is a classic of Alsace and Switzerland) until my first meal at Fredy Girardet's in Crissier, Switzerland, which many people consider to be the finest restaurant in the world. Chef Girardet himself brought forth an extra course, this simple quiche. As I was anxiously awaiting my initiation to some of the world's great gustatory delights I was a bit annoyed that my appetite, carefully prepared with much starvation, might be lessened by a common tart. But with Chef Girardet standing over me I could hardly refrain. What a revelation! This is not his recipe, but it is close, and I think you will find that it handsomely rewards your efforts.

The only difficulty with this quiche is cooking the onions. The French have a saying that a good cook is someone who "knows his (or her) onions." You'll understand it once you've done it properly.

**8-inch prebaked quiche shell
(see pages 25 and 26)**
7 tablespoons unsalted butter
2 pounds onions, sliced
2 tablespoons safflower oil
2 tablespoons flour
3 large eggs
1 cup heavy cream
**3 ounces Gruyère cheese, freshly
grated**

Preheat the oven to 375 degrees.

Dice 3 tablespoons of butter and refrigerate.

In a large sauté pan cook the onions in the remaining butter and the oil, starting over medium heat and gradually reducing to low heat, for about 1 hour, until the onions are very tender, golden and reduced considerably in size. Stir continuously for the last 15 minutes and be very careful not to let them burn. They will be extraordinarily sweet and delectable. Discard any burned parts. Sprinkle the onions with the flour, using a strainer or a sifter, and sauté another 2 or 3 minutes.

Beat the eggs and cream in a bowl with a third of the cheese. Stir in the onions, then pour the mixture into the quiche shell. Sprinkle with the remaining cheese and dot with the diced butter. Bake 25 to 35 minutes, or until browned and set.

Curry Quiche

This rather substantial quiche is definitely for the main course of a lunch or light dinner, and is designed to use up leftovers—shrimp, chicken, turkey, lamb or whatever. You can vary the amount of shrimp or fowl or meat used by adjusting the amount of rice: There should be two cups of the two altogether. The idea for including the chutney right in the quiche comes from a friend, Charlie Bergman, who puts chutney in a very good curried chicken salad that he serves at parties.

And apologies to Madhur Jaffrey and Julie Sahni: Certainly curry powder will never produce an authentic Indian *curry, but it has become an important flavoring ingredient on its own in American, English and French kitchens.*

**10-inch prebaked quiche shell
  (see pages 25 and 26)**
1 tablespoon salt
⅓ cup long-grain rice
3 tablespoons unsalted butter
½ cup chopped onions
1½ tablespoons curry powder
3 large eggs
1½ cups heavy cream
½ teaspoon salt
3-4 tablespoons minced chutney
**1 cup cooked shrimp or chopped
  chicken, turkey, lamb, beef, etc.**

Preheat the oven to 375 degrees.

Heat 2 quarts of water to boiling, add 1 tablespoon of salt to the boiling water and pour in the rice. Remove the rice after 12 minutes by pouring it through a strainer.

Melt 1 tablespoon of the butter in a sauté pan over medium heat, add the onions and sauté about 5 minutes until they are translucent but not browned. Add the rest of the butter and, as soon as it's melted, add the curry powder. Stir continually for about 2 minutes.

Beat the eggs with the cream and add the onion-curry mixture (using some cream to rinse out the pan and get all of the curry). Stir in the rice and remaining ingredients. Pour into the quiche shell and bake for 25 to 35 minutes, until puffed and golden.

This quiche reheats quite nicely.

Shrimp (or Seafood) Quiche

The delicious flavor of this quiche makes it a general favorite. Once I used it as an hors d'oeuvre at a cocktail party, baking a rectangular pastry shell, then cutting it into small squares. It disappeared almost instantly.

Taking the trouble to work with fresh shrimp as outlined below will result in a superior flavor. If fresh shrimp are not available, then use frozen (never canned), defrosting them very slowly and sautéing them briefly with the shallots. Of course crab, crayfish or lobster may be substituted with equally good results.

**8-inch prebaked quiche shell
(see pages 25 and 26)
6 ounces small fresh shrimp
½ cup dry white wine
½ bay leaf
¼ teaspoon thyme
6 tablespoons unsalted butter
3 tablespoons minced shallots
3 tablespoons Madeira or port
Salt and freshly ground pepper
to taste
3 large eggs
1 cup heavy cream
2 tablespoons tomato paste
2 ounces Gruyère cheese, freshly
grated**

Preheat the oven to 375 degrees.

Rinse the shrimp but do not peel them. Place the wine, bay leaf and thyme in a saucepan just large enough to hold the shrimp. Add 1 to 2 cups of water, just enough to comfortably cover the shrimp. Heat to boiling, then reduce the heat and simmer, covered, 5 to 10 minutes, *without the shrimp*. Add the shrimp and simmer, *uncovered*, until they turn pink, about 1 to 2 minutes at most. Remove from heat and let cool in the liquid. When the shrimp are cool, shell them, *reserving the shells*. If the shrimp are large, cut them in half or thirds.

Melt 4 tablespoons of the butter and pour it into a blender, then add the shrimp shells. Blend, turning on and off and scraping down the sides frequently. Add more melted butter if needed. When thoroughly blended, strain through a fine sieve, mashing down on the shells to get as much of the butter through the sieve as possible. Discard the shells and chill the shrimp butter.

Sauté the shallots in the remaining butter until translucent but not browned, about 2 minutes. Add the wine, salt and pepper and shrimp and sauté gently 2 to 3 minutes, just enough to warm the shrimp and evaporate the raw alcohol from the wine.

Beat the eggs with the cream and tomato paste in a bowl. Mix the shrimp in, then pour everything into the quiche shell. Sprinkle with cheese and dot with the chilled shrimp butter. Bake 25 to 35 minutes, or until browned and set.

Simca's Tomato Quiche

One of my first visits to Bramafan, Simca's home near Cannes, was on a hot summer day in the early 1970s. When I arrived, lunch was waiting on the long, shady stone terrace that runs the length of the old Provençal farmhouse. The simple table was proudly set with white-tipped radishes fresh from the garden, crusty local bread and sweet butter, shiny black olives from the trees above and around us, miniature green beans in vinaigrette, barely blanched and bursting with flavor, and this fine tomato quiche, filled with the warm rich scents of the hills of southern France.

Be certain your tomatoes are full of flavor. If you can't get them vine-picked and in season, perhaps organically grown, use a good imported Italian canned tomato. If you use the tasteless out-of-season supermarket beauties or even some of the home-grown hybrid varieties with their hearty skins, great color, disease resistance and lack of flavor, you'll never know the fragrant tastes of Provence.

If your thyme and oregano have been sitting on the shelf too long, you may have to use much more than the teaspoon called for. Taste before baking and demand a rich, deep tomato flavor with strong Mediterranean scents.

8-inch prebaked quiche shell
  (see pages 25 and 26)
3 tablespoons unsalted butter
3 tablespoons olive oil
½ pound onions, coarsely chopped
2 pounds ripe tomatoes or 1 cup
  canned Italian tomatoes
1 teaspoon thyme
1 teaspoon oregano
2 teaspoons salt
½ teaspoon freshly ground pepper
2 large eggs
1 cup heavy cream
½ cup freshly grated Parmesan
  cheese

Preheat the oven to 375 degrees.

Melt the butter with the oil in a large sauté pan and cook the onions slowly for 15 to 20 minutes over medium heat until they begin to brown.

Meanwhile, if you are using fresh tomatoes, drop them in 1 quart of boiling water for 5 seconds, then peel them. (If the skins do not come off easily they are not really ripe enough; give them another 15 seconds in the boiling water.) Cut the peeled tomatoes in half horizontally and squeeze the seeds and juices out. Chop coarsely and cook in another saucepan, about 10 to 15 minutes over medium heat, until you have a thick puree with all the water evaporated. Season with thyme, oregano, salt and pepper.

Add the onions to the tomatoes, then stir in the eggs beaten lightly with the cream. Fill the quiche shell about three quarters full, sprinkle with the cheese and bake for 25 to 35 minutes, or until nicely browned and set. Let cool a bit before serving.

This may be reheated.

Two-Mushroom Quiche

The wild mushrooms available in our market in Innsbruck, Austria, are truly amazing; sometimes we see a fungus for sale that we've never seen or heard of before. We buy it, take it home and clean it, perhaps sauté it with butter and then add some cream or maybe just some parsley and garlic. The taste can be exotic, sensual or both, and the textures have enormous variety as well. And the sizes! I've seen a mushroom with the circumference of an inner tube; the vendor cuts off slices and sells them to be sautéed like a steak.

A larger variety of mushrooms is beginning to become available in New York, which usually means that soon the same thing will happen around the country, especially if people ask for them. If you can find only cultivated mushrooms in your local stores, send for some dried wild mushrooms. The large, dark Chinese mushrooms can be interesting, but they're very strong. Almost any wild mushrooms from Europe are excellent. I look forward to the day when we'll see our own excellent wild mushrooms in American supermarkets.

**8-inch prebaked quiche shell
(see pages 25 and 26)**
½ pound cultivated mushrooms
**½ pound wild mushrooms, or
2 ounces dried wild mushrooms
(cèpes or porcini, chanterelles,
etc.)**
3-4 tablespoons minced shallots
2 tablespoons unsalted butter
4 tablespoons port or Madeira wine
1 teaspoon salt
¼ teaspoon freshly ground pepper
**4 tablespoons minced fresh parsley
(or 2 tablespoons minced fresh
tarragon and 2 tablespoons
parsley)**
2 large eggs
1 cup heavy cream

Preheat the oven to 375 degrees.

Wipe the cultivated mushrooms with a damp cloth to remove grit, slice a thin layer off the stems, and cut in ¼-inch lengthwise slices. (A food processor does this very nicely.) Wash the wild mushrooms, dry them in a salad spinner and prepare like the cultivated ones. If you are using dried mushrooms, put them in a bowl with boiling water to cover and let sit 20 minutes. Drain, then cover with cold water and drain again; repeat several times until the water runs almost clear. Prepare by cutting in lengthwise slices.

Sauté the shallots in butter over medium heat for about 2 minutes without letting them brown. Add the mushrooms and continue sautéing for about 8 to 10 minutes. The mushrooms will absorb all the liquid, then they will release it together with their juices, next the liquid will evaporate and finally the mushrooms will begin to brown.

Add the wine and cook 2 to 3 minutes until it is almost completely absorbed. Add salt and pepper to taste, then the parsley.

Stir in the eggs, beaten lightly with the cream, and pour the mixture into the quiche shell. Bake for 25 to 35 minutes, or until nicely browned and set. Cool a bit before serving.

Zucchini, Cream and Tarragon Quiche

Zucchini, when it is not overcooked and tastes like itself, is a vegetable that almost everyone likes. This quiche makes an excellent first course or a fine accompaniment to almost any main course, if cooked as a gratin, without a crust, in a buttered baking dish.

Richard Olney, one of the most creative cooks of our era, originated this treatment for zucchini. Select small, firm zucchini and measure the salt carefully. Be certain to use unsalted butter—no margarine or oil—and fragrant tarragon. (I always unscrew the top of the bottle and smell the herb before buying—no smell, no taste, no purchase.) If shallots aren't available, use the white bulbs of scallions or spring onions, or even a small white onion. The taste will fully reward your efforts.

8-inch prebaked quiche shell
  (see pages 25 and 26)
6 tablespoons unsalted butter
2 pounds zucchini
2 teaspoons salt
4 ounces fresh cream cheese
½ cup heavy cream
2 large eggs
2 teaspoons dried tarragon
4 shallots, minced
Freshly ground pepper
½ cup freshly grated Gruyère cheese

Preheat the oven to 375 degrees.

Cut 2 tablespoons of butter into dice and refrigerate.

Scrub the zucchini well to remove any grit, cut off both ends and grate with the skin on, using a food processor or the coarse part of a hand grater. Toss with the salt and place in a colander to drain for 20 to 30 minutes.

Meanwhile mix the cream cheese and cream with the eggs and add the tarragon; set aside so that the tarragon can begin infusing the mixture with flavor.

Sauté the shallots in 2 tablespoons of the remaining butter for 2 to 3 minutes, not letting them brown.

Squeeze the zucchini dry with your hands and taste it: If it's too salty, rinse and squeeze dry again. Then sauté it with the shallots and remaining butter for 3 to 4 minutes, not letting it brown. Season to taste with pepper. Stir the cream-egg mixture into the zucchini and fill the quiche shell about three-quarters full. Sprinkle with the cheese, dot with the diced cold butter and bake 25 to 35 minutes, or until crusty and brown.

Tuna Quiche Oregano

Serves 4-6

The marriage of oregano with tuna (salmon may also be used with equal success) is unexpected and quite delicious. This hearty quiche is perhaps best served as a main course for lunch with a nice green salad and a bottle of dry white wine.

Be certain to use flavorful oregano (its cousin marjoram may be substituted), and preferably the leaf variety rather than the powdered. Use your favorite brand of tuna, but not one packed in water. White or dark meat will make little difference.

9-inch prebaked quiche shell (see pages 25 and 26)
4 tablespoons unsalted butter
4 tablespoons chopped onions
1-2 teaspoons dried oregano
2 6½- or 7-ounce cans tuna
Juices from tuna cans plus enough heavy cream to make 1 cup
2 large eggs
1 teaspoon salt
¼ teaspoon freshly ground black pepper
2 tablespoons tomato paste
2 tablespoons minced fresh parsley
¾ cup freshly grated Gruyère cheese

Preheat the oven to 375 degrees.

Melt the butter, add the onions and sauté for about 5 minutes over medium heat until translucent but not browned. Add the oregano and sauté it, stirring continuously, for 1 minute.

Drain the tuna, reserving the juices, and break it up coarsely in a bowl. Beat the juices and cream with the eggs until mixed and add it to the tuna. Add the onion-oregano mixture, salt, pepper, tomato paste, parsley and half of the cheese. Mix well and taste for seasoning. Pour into the quiche shell, sprinkle the remaining cheese over the quiche and bake for 25 to 35 minutes or until set. Let cool 5 to 10 minutes before serving.

Mussel Quiche

Serves 8

Mussels are certainly one of the earth's great natural resources because they are readily available in natural or cultivated states. It's strange that more Americans are not familiar with them because they're one of the few seafood bargains left, and certainly one of the tastiest. Luckily they're likely to remain so, because as more and more people discover what Europeans have treasured for years as a delicacy, our production of them becomes more efficient.

All the American cookbooks I've come across, and even the French cookbooks printed in this country, tell you to soak mussels for a minimum of an hour to rid them of any sand or grit. When Jacques Cagna was visiting one of my classes he was astonished. "We never soak them," he said. "In fact, we have a saying: 'You're exchanging the sea water for tap water. Which do you prefer?'" He was indeed right: Sea water yields much more flavor. When I asked him about removal of grit he laughed and turned the question around: "In spite of whatever precautions and soakings, have you ever had mussels without some grit?" I had to admit I hadn't. So down with all the editors who have been "correcting" those French cookbooks and robbing mussel dishes of their flavor.

**10-inch prebaked quiche shell
  (see pages 25 and 26)**
30 small mussels
½ cup dry white wine
1 teaspoon dried thyme
½ bay leaf
**4 tablespoons minced shallots
  or onions**
2 tablespoons butter
1 cup heavy cream
3 large eggs
4 tablespoons minced fresh parsley
Freshly ground black pepper

Preheat the oven to 375 degrees.

Scrub the mussels well with a stiff brush or by rubbing one against the other to remove dirt and barnacles, and pull off the "beard" coming out of the shell. If any are open, tap them sharply. If they close, however sluggishly, they're still alive; if not discard them. Rinse thoroughly.

Place the mussels with the wine, thyme and bay leaf in a casserole with a tight-fitting cover and cook over medium heat. Check in 3 minutes—as soon as the shells open remove the mussels. Give any recalcitrant mussels plenty of chance to open as stubborn ones are often the most alive and thus the tastiest. Discard those that don't open. Let them cool while you're straining all the liquid through a double layer of cheesecloth to remove the grit, then reduce it down to ⅓ to ½ cup. Remove mussels from the shells; discard shells.

Meanwhile sauté the shallots or onions in the butter and heat the cream and the eggs in a bowl. Shallots are sautéed 1 to 2 minutes, onion about 5, in both cases until translucent but not brown. Put the shallots or onions into the egg-cream mixture and add the reduced mussel cooking liquids and parsley. Taste for seasoning; little if any salt should be needed but you will probably want a little pepper.

Place the mussels around the quiche shell, pour the cream mixture over it and bake 25 to 35 minutes, or until browned and set.

Serve as a first course or entree with a nice dry white wine such as a Muscadet.

NOTE: If mussels are unavailable, clams or oysters may be substituted or you can use canned mussels if they are "natural," not smoked or treated. If you do use canned mussels, drain them reserving the liquid, combine the liquid with ½ cup white wine and reduce to ⅓ to ½ cup with the thyme and bay leaf. Then proceed as above. You do lose some of the honest flavors of the sea this way, but the result is close enough to be worth the effort.

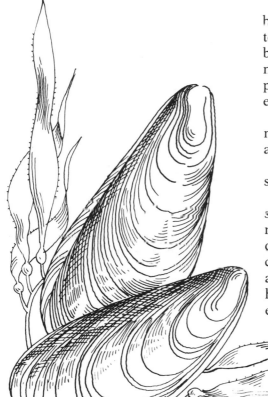

Cucumber and Dill Quiche

The tangy combination of cucumbers, fresh dill and cream turns into a delightfully light and delicate quiche, to precede a summer dinner on the terrace or a hot and robust dinner on a cold night.

The amount of cucumbers may appear to be excessive, but they will shrink a great deal when they lose their large amount of water. The salting, draining and then sautéing will concentrate the cucumber flavor, as will using the skin—which also lends color.

**9-inch prebaked quiche shell
(see pages 25 and 26)**
4 medium-size cucumbers
3 teaspoons salt
1 cup heavy cream
½ cup chopped onions
3 tablespoons unsalted butter
1 teaspoon white wine vinegar
2 large eggs
4 tablespoons minced fresh dill

Preheat the oven to 375 degrees.

Wash the cucumbers carefully to remove any sprays or wax—scrub with hot water if necessary. Peel the cucumbers, reserving the skins. Cut them lengthwise, then run a teaspoon down the centers to remove all seeds. Grate the cucumbers by hand or in a food processor, sprinkle with salt and let drain in a sieve for 20 to 30 minutes.

Put the cucumber peels and the cream in a saucepan over medium heat and simmer for 5 to 10 minutes until the cream tastes of cucumber. Put the cream and peels in a blender and blend until the peels are completely pureed, then pass them through a fine strainer to remove any coarse bits.

Sauté the onions in the butter for about 5 minutes until translucent, but do not let them brown.

Squeeze the cucumbers with your hands to remove excess water, pat them dry with paper towels, then add to the onions and sauté several minutes until they begin to brown and any water is evaporated. Add the vinegar and turn off the heat.

Mix everything together, making certain that the eggs are well beaten and that there is at least 1 cup of cream (if not, add more, or yogurt). Add the dill. Pour into the quiche shell and bake 25 to 35 minutes, or until set and browned on top. Serve right away.

Quiche of Baby Peas and Smoked Ham

The combination of peas cooked with well-smoked ham and a hint of garlic is a very special taste which I was introduced to some years back by Marcella Hazan. I found that when it was put into a quiche it took on new dimensions. This quiche is very successful as a first course or as a complement to an entree, but make certain that the entree is outstanding or this Italian-French hybrid will surprise you and walk off with all the honors.

Unless you can find fresh, unshelled baby peas just a few days off the vine (which is almost impossible) I would recommend frozen baby peas. But don't follow the directions on the package for this (or any other) recipe; merely defrost them either under cold running water or by letting them sit out. The ham is best if it's double smoked. Or use Italian prosciutto, if it's available. Don't use tasteless boiled ham or you'll be wasting your time.

9½-inch prebaked quiche shell
  (see pages 25 and 26)
4 ounces double-smoked ham in
  ⅛-inch slices
10 ounces (1 package) frozen
  baby peas
1 tablespoon unsalted butter
1 clove garlic, minced
1 cup heavy cream
2 large eggs
2 ounces Gruyère cheese, freshly
  grated

Preheat the oven to 375 degrees.

Cut the ham into ⅛-inch dice, including any fat. Defrost the peas under cold running water or by letting them sit out.

Sauté the ham in the butter over medium heat. When the ham is browning nicely, add the garlic and continue to sauté for another minute, stirring continually so that the garlic does not burn.

Beat the cream and eggs together in another bowl, add the ham-garlic mixture and the peas, stir well, then pour into the quiche shell. Sprinkle with the cheese and place in the oven for 25 to 35 minutes, or until nicely browned and set.

Italian Beet Quiche

I'm particularly fond of beets, and this quiche incorporates one of my favorite combinations, beets cooked with heavy cream and butter, topped with the special richness of real Parmesan cheese. I found this delectable idea in an old Italian cookbook with recipes from the 18th century and it has become one of my favorite ways with beets.

Beets are best when fresh, although they certainly are one of the better vegetables for canning. Marion Cunningham, our "new Fannie Farmer," showed me her method of cooking fresh ones. It is so easy and makes the beets taste so good that I can't see any reason other than lack of fresh beets for not using it always.

9½-inch prebaked quiche shell
  (see pages 25 and 26)
3-4 medium-size beets or 2 cups
  grated beets
4 tablespoons unsalted butter
½ teaspoon salt
¼ teaspoon freshly ground black
  pepper
1 cup heavy cream
2 large eggs
1 cup freshly grated Parmesan
  cheese

Preheat the oven to 350 degrees.

Place the beets on aluminum foil in the oven for about 2 hours or until a toothpick goes in easily. (Larger beets can take twice as long.) Cool, then peel them; the skins will come off easily. Grate the beets by hand or in a food processor, reserving 2 cups for the quiche; any excess will make a delicious salad.

Turn the oven up to 375 degrees.

Sauté the beets in the butter for 2 to 3 minutes over medium heat. Season with the salt and pepper.

Beat the cream with the eggs in a bowl, then stir in the beets and a third of the cheese. Pour into the quiche shell, sprinkle with the remaining cheese, and bake for 25 to 35 minutes or until set.

Rum Cheese Quiche

Serves 4-6

Perhaps the most popular French dessert quiche is one made with cheese, but it seems rather bland to American palates, used to our heavy cheesecakes. This variation adds a nice rum flavor and includes raisins for a textural and color contrast. The quiche is equally delicious in a sweet pastry shell or baked without a crust in individual ramekins or custard cups, if you need a quick dessert.

Be certain to use a flavorful dark rum. I usually use a Jamaican rum but there are others that are very good. As always, the cream cheese should be fresh, not one with gums and preservatives, or you won't be able to get the best rich flavor.

**8-inch prebaked sweet quiche shell
   (see pages 27 and 28)**
½ cup raisins
½ cup dark rum
4 ounces fresh cream cheese
½ cup heavy cream
**8 tablespoons unsalted butter, at
   room temperature**
1 cup sugar
3 large eggs

Preheat the oven to 375 degrees.

Put the raisins and the rum in a small saucepan and simmer 3 to 4 minutes to get rid of the raw alcohol taste in the rum and to plump the raisins.

Meanwhile cream the cheese, cream and butter until smooth in a food processor or with an electric hand beater. Then add the sugar and eggs and beat again to obtain a smooth, lump-free mixture. Add the rum and raisins, stir again, pour into the quiche shell and bake for 25 to 35 minutes, or until puffed and set. (If you are using individual baking dishes, about 20 minutes is sufficient.)

Cinnamon Prune Quiche

Anyone who has a "thing" about prunes and just can't imagine having a prune quiche for dessert is going to be missing one of the better dishes in this little book. The original idea came in the form of a gift from André Daguin of prunes canned in a cinnamon syrup. Daguin's two-star Michelin-rated restaurant in the Hotel de France in Auch is worth the drive down to the southwestern corner of the country. Prunes and cinnamon are a delightful combination, and when cooked in Madeira and combined with cream, this marriage is indeed blessed.

The major expense will be the cinnamon sticks. Ground cinnamon can be substituted, but you certainly won't get the same delectable taste as when the cream and milk have been thoroughly infused. I think you'll find it a worthwhile indulgence.

**9-inch prebaked quiche shell
  (see pages 25 to 28)**
⅓ cup slivered almonds
¾ cup pitted prunes
¾ cup Madeira
1 cup heavy cream
1 cup milk
10 short cinnamon sticks
3 large eggs
¾ cup sugar
Whipped cream (optional)

Preheat the oven to 375 degrees.

As the oven is heating, toast the slivered almonds on a baking sheet. Be careful not to let them burn.

Put the prunes and Madeira in a saucepan over medium heat and simmer until the Madeira is a syrupy glaze of 2 to 3 tablespoons.

Meanwhile combine the cream and milk in another saucepan, crumble the cinnamon sticks into it and simmer for about 15 minutes.

When the cream-milk mixture is well infused (taste it), pour it into a blender and blend about 2 minutes, until the mixture turns a rich cinnamon color. Strain through a very fine sieve *without* pressing down on the cinnamon sticks. Discard the cinnamon sticks.

Beat the eggs and sugar together in a bowl until they are creamy and a pale yellow color, then mix in the cream-milk infusion.

Cut the prunes in half lengthwise and place them around the quiche shell. Carefully scrape all the reduced Madeira into the cream-milk mixture and blend it in. Pour over the prunes and bake 20 minutes.

Remove the quiche and shut the oven door quickly. Place the toasted slivered almonds around the top, then return to the oven for another 5 to 10 minutes, or until set.

Though the quiche is quite rich on its own, it is very well complemented with *unsweetened* freshly whipped cream spooned or piped through a pastry bag around the top just before serving.

Lemon Quiche

The tart, refreshing lemon is a favorite ingredient for dessert, pleasing to most palates and acceptable after almost any entree. It's been one of my personal favorites ever since I had my first lemon mousse in a tiny bistro when I was about 10 years old. I've been trying to recreate that mousse ever since. Luckily I never have, for the attempt keeps me thinking of new lemon-based desserts.

The zest of the lemon contains so much lemon oil that it has more flavor than the juice. Infusing the milk and cream helps develop a rich lemony flavor which complements the thick custardy taste of this quiche.

**10-inch prebaked quiche shell
  (see pages 25 to 28)**
4 lemons
1 cup heavy cream
1 cup milk
½ cup sugar
2 large eggs plus 2 yolks
1 teaspoon flour

Preheat the oven to 375 degrees.

Zest one lemon by using the smallest side of a hand grater over some wax paper. Then run a toothpick in diagonal directions to remove all the lemon from the sharp front of the grater. Your hand can get the bits that adhere to the back. Place the zest in a saucepan with the cream and milk and simmer gently for 5 minutes.

Juice all the lemons, including the zested one, and strain.

With an electric mixer, beat the sugar with the eggs and yolks until the mixture turns lemony yellow, then add the flour and beat some more to incorporate smoothly. Mix in the milk-cream infusion and lemon juice, and pour into the quiche shell.

Bake for 25 to 35 minutes, or until puffed and set.

NOTE: If you wish to decorate the quiche, use a swivel-edge vegetable peeler and take off several long pieces of zest from the lemons you haven't zested. Cut these pieces into fine julienne strips. Cook 3 tablespoons of sugar in ½ cup water for 5 minutes, add the lemon strips and cook 10 minutes, or until they've lost their bitter taste and are candied. (Do *not* taste while hot from the sugar syrup.) Remove and let them dry on a rack. Arrange on the lemon quiche before serving

Apple Cinnamon Quiche

This is a dessert for winter or late fall, when apples are crisp, nights are cold, and our desire for something warm, sweet and reassuring makes us overlook the calories. These are the tastes of Normandy: rich, thick cream, sweet butter and tart, juicy apples.

Select crisp, tart apples such as Granny Smiths or greenings, use crème fraîche if you can, and be certain the butter used is sweet and delicious.

10-inch prebaked quiche shell
  (see pages 25 to 28)
⅓ cup almonds, unpeeled
⅓ cup sugar
2 tablespoons water
Pinch cream of tartar
1½ cups crème fraîche or heavy
  cream
4 cinnamon sticks, about 4 inches
  long
2 crisp green apples
½ lemon, juiced
1 cup sugar
2 large eggs
⅓ cup raisins
2 tablespoons unsalted butter, diced
  and chilled
Whipped cream or vanilla ice cream
  (optional)

Preheat the oven to 375 degrees.

Drop the almonds in boiling water for 45 seconds, remove and rub roughly in a dish towel as soon as they are cool enough to touch. Some skins will come off; using your thumb and index finger, squeeze or pinch the remaining almonds to remove their skins. Then place them on a lightly oiled baking sheet and put them in the oven for about 8 minutes to dry them thoroughly and toast them slightly.

Meanwhile put the sugar in a small saucepan (not copper) with 2 tablespoons of water and a pinch of cream of tartar (if you have none, use a teaspoon of corn syrup or a few drops of lemon juice) and heat to boiling. Let boil for about 10 minutes until it begins to color an even light brown. Remove the nuts from the oven (they should be warm) and, using a wooden spoon, stir them into the caramel to coat them all over. Immediately pour them out onto an oiled baking sheet and spread them out flat, using the spoon or an orange or lemon. Let them harden (about 10 minutes).

Infuse the cream by bringing it to a simmer with the cinnamon sticks crumbled in it and cooking about 5 minutes. Pour the cream and cinnamon into a blender or food processor and blend for several minutes, until the cream is colored and the cinnamon well ground. Strain through a fine sieve *without* pressing down on the cinnamon. Discard the cinnamon.

Peel the apples, then coarsely grate them into a bowl with a hand grater without coring or quartering them. Discard the core and seeds. Sprinkle with the lemon juice and toss.

Beat the sugar with the eggs in another bowl until it is very pale yellow, then add the raisins, apples and cream and stir again. Pour into the quiche shell, dot with the chilled butter and bake for 20 to 30 minutes, or until *almost* set. Remove from oven.

While the quiche is baking, roughly chop the nougatine (almonds in hardened caramel) with a knife into small pieces. After removing the quiche from the oven, sprinkle it with the nougatine and bake again until puffed and golden. Wait about 15 minutes before serving.

If you wish, serve this with sweetened whipped cream or vanilla ice cream.

Peach and Pepper Quiche

Serves 4-6

André Daguin was also the inspiration for this fascinating combination of flavors. Unlikely as it may seem, the pepper ends up as only a subtle hint, but one that brings forth the essence of the peach.

Finding a good peach poses a real problem, like finding a good tomato. If you can find really succulent peaches with that captured sunshine, then make this quiche.

9-inch prebaked quiche shell
  (see pages 25 to 28)
1½ cups dry red wine
1 cup plus 1 tablespoon sugar
2 tablespoons peppercorns
4 medium-size peaches
3 large eggs
1 tablespoon flour
1 cup heavy cream
Whipped cream or vanilla ice cream
  (optional)

Preheat the oven to 375 degrees. Put a small pot of water on to boil.

In a small saucepan with a cover heat the wine, ½ cup plus 1 tablespoon of sugar and the peppercorns to boiling, then reduce the heat, cover and simmer about 5 minutes.

Meanwhile dip the peaches in the boiling water for 15 to 25 seconds each, then remove and peel them. Cut each peach into slices. When the wine syrup is ready, add the peaches and poach until tender, from 5 to 25 minutes depending on their ripeness.

Beat the eggs with the remaining ½ cup sugar in a bowl until they are a very light, creamy yellow, then add the flour and beat some more, and finally the heavy cream.

When the peaches are poached, remove them from the liquid and reduce the liquid to about ½ cup. Strain it to remove the peppercorns and add it to the egg-cream mixture. Wipe or rinse off any pepper from the peaches and place them around the quiche shell. Pour the egg-cream mixture over and bake 25 to 35 minutes, or until puffed and set.

If you wish, serve with sweetened whipped cream or vanilla ice cream.

Hazelnut Delight Quiche

My son Christopher, who helped test many of the recipes in this book and who is a cook in his own right, came up with the idea for this luscious nut quiche. Hazelnuts, also known as filberts, have not yet come into their own in America. In Europe they are one of the most popular tastes, along with chocolate and vanilla. I suspect that they will become a favorite for you after a mouthful or two of this rich quiche.

Look for hazelnuts in health food stores if they are not readily available in your supermarket. You can buy them already peeled, which will save you a lot of trouble, but like all nuts they'll be fresher if you peel them yourself. Some health food stores have grinders for making nut butters—this would be a quite acceptable way to simplify this recipe.

10-inch prebaked quiche shell
  (see pages 25 to 28)
1½ cups hazelnuts
1¼ cups granulated sugar
3 tablespoons water
Pinch of cream of tartar
1-2 tablespoons oil
1½ cups heavy cream
2 large eggs
2 tablespoons confectioners' sugar
½ teaspoon vanilla

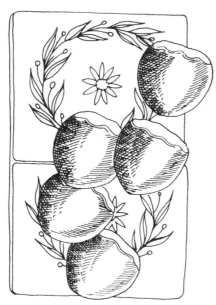

Preheat the oven to 375 degrees.

Place the hazelnuts on a tray in the oven for about 10 minutes. Do not let them burn. Take them out and rub them vigorously with a clean dish towel to remove their skins; when they are cool enough, roughly rub the stubborn ones in your hands, a handful at a time. It is not necessary to remove all of the skins, but they tend to impart an off taste. Keep ½ cup of the nuts warm.

In a stainless steel or aluminum saucepan, heat ½ cup of the sugar and 3 tablespoons of water to boiling. Add a pinch of cream of tartar (if you have none, 1 teaspoon of corn syrup or a few drops of white vinegar will also do) and continue cooking to a light brown color.

Meanwhile lightly oil a baking sheet with 1 to 2 tablespoons of oil. When the syrup is a light brown, pour the ½ cup of warmed nuts into it and stir with a wooden spoon to coat the nuts evenly. Immediately pour them out onto the oiled baking sheet. Flatten them as much as you can (an orange or lemon is good for this, because the oil in the skins does not stick to the caramel), and let cool, about 10 minutes.

Grind the remaining nuts with the rest of the sugar in a food processor to form nut butter: This will take from 6 to 10 minutes. The food processor may have to be scraped down from time to time, but the oils must emerge and it must be somewhat like a peanut butter.

When the nougatine (hazelnuts in caramel) has cooled and hardened, chop it coarsely with a knife into pieces small enough to eat.

Mix 1 cup of cream and the eggs together, add to the nut

butter and pour into a quiche shell. Sprinkle the nougatine over the top. Bake 25 to 35 minutes until browned and set.

Meanwhile whip the rest of the cream in a chilled bowl or over ice until soft peaks form (when the bowl is tilted they will move). Then add the confectioners' sugar and vanilla and beat just to stiff peaks (they will not move when the bowl is tilted). Refrigerate until ready to use.

Serve the quiche tepid with dollops of whipped cream placed on the top with a large tablespoon or piped through a pastry bag.

Brown and White Banana Quiche

Serves 6

Bananas please almost everyone and are available with dependable consistency the year round. This warm, comforting banana custard glazed with brown sugar and topped with whipped cream should soothe all.

Look for bananas with "freckles," a sign that they're in a perfect stage of ripeness for eating and rich with flavor. If you can't find them in that condition, keep them out of the refrigerator for a few days until they ripen to perfection.

**9-inch prebaked quiche shell
  (see pages 25 to 28)
4 bananas (about 1½ pounds
  unpeeled)
2 large eggs, beaten
1 tablespoon dark rum
¼ teaspoon ground cinnamon
½ teaspoon vanilla
4 tablespoons sugar
1½ cups heavy cream
½ cup milk
4-6 tablespoons dark brown sugar
Whipped cream (optional)**

Preheat the oven to 375 degrees.

Peel 3 of the bananas and puree them in a food processor, then measure out 2 cups and place in a bowl. Add the eggs, rum, cinnamon, vanilla, sugar, ½ cup of the cream and the milk, and mix well. Fill the quiche shell and bake 20 to 25 minutes, or until *almost* set.

Meanwhile whip the remaining cream in a chilled bowl until stiff. If you do this ahead of time (you can do it as much as a day in advance, which results in firmer whipped cream), place the whipped cream in a cheesecloth-lined sieve or strainer over a dish to catch the excess liquid, and refrigerate.

Slice the remaining banana. Remove the quiche from the oven and place the slices all around the top. Sprinkle with brown sugar and return to the oven for 5 to 10 minutes, or until nicely set and browned. Don't let the sugar burn. Remove the quiche and cool to tepid.

Before serving, put dollops of whipped cream, sweetened or not, as you wish, around the quiche, using a large tablespoon or piping it through a pastry bag with a star tip.

Miller's Quiche (*Quiche Meunière*)

Meunière, a term often seen in cookbooks and on menus, means a miller's wife; applied to food it usually means dusted with flour. However, in this quiche it represents a variation of an old recipe from my mother's family, the Millers. The quiche is very hearty and rich, good for cold winter nights when you will want to top it with an even richer buttery hard sauce. It's a quiche for friends who are carrot cake fanciers, but few will ever know that potatoes also play an important part, along with ground almonds.

Generally fresh almonds, blanched and peeled, have the most taste (the skins preserve the freshness of the oils), but it will be hard to discern in this case. If you wish to use fresh ones, see the Ingredients section. As this quiche is rather substantial, it works equally well without the quiche shell.

10-inch prebaked quiche shell
  (see pages 25 to 28)
2 cups grated carrots
2 cups grated potatoes
¼ cup raisins
Cognac (optional)
½ cup blanched almonds
2 large eggs
1 cup sugar
1 cup heavy cream
1 teaspoon vanilla
½ teaspoon cinnamon
¼ teaspoon allspice
2 tablespoons unsalted butter, diced
  and chilled
3 tablespoons dark brown sugar
Sweetened whipped cream
  (optional)

Preheat the oven to 375 degrees.

Blanch the carrots and potatoes in 3 to 4 quarts of boiling salted water for 5 minutes. Drain and let drip through a sieve to remove excess water; press down on them a bit.

Meanwhile steep the raisins in boiling water (or better, in warm Cognac to cover) if they are at all dry or stiff. Pulverize the almonds into a fine powder using a blender or food processor.

Beat the eggs with the sugar until they are creamy and light yellow in color, then beat in the cream, vanilla, cinnamon and allspice. Stir in the drained raisins, carrots and potatoes, then the almonds, and pour the mixture into the quiche shell. Dot with the chilled butter and bake 25 to 35 minutes, or until puffed and set.

Turn the oven up to 450 degrees.

Just before serving, sprinkle the brown sugar over the top of the quiche and return to the oven to melt and caramelize the sugar, about 4 to 5 minutes.

NOTE: This is delicious by itself, served with slightly sweetened whipped cream or with a hard sauce.

HARD SAUCE

8 tablespoons unsalted butter,
  softened
1 cup confectioners' sugar
Rum, Cognac or other liqueur,
  to taste

With a hand mixer, cream the butter with the sugar, then add liqueur to taste, tablespoon by tablespoon. Chill about half an hour but do not let it get truly hard.

Pâté

About Pâtés

In a sense, a pâté is nothing more than an elegant meatloaf. Little more equipment is needed than a loaf pan of some sort (even the heavy aluminum foil kind available in most supermarkets is quite satisfactory) and some aluminum foil to cover. True, the French have refined the art of pâté-making to a high level, and there are pâtés that can be considered quite difficult and challenging for the novice, such as the Rabbit Pâté in this book. But many are simplicity itself, can be turned out in minutes, and are well within the capabilities of true beginners. Furthermore, even the most complicated pâté can be made in a simplified version with little loss of taste.

What's the difference between a meatloaf and a pâté? Well, very little. Flavor and taste, mostly, and the way you get them. In a meatloaf we generally use hamburger, which is perhaps the least interesting of meats to use when it must be cooked as long as a meatloaf or pâté requires. Generally extenders are added, perhaps cornflakes or breadcrumbs, neither of which contributes much in the way of flavor. Chopped raw onions or celery might be included, and ketchup is sometimes placed on the bottom of the pan and strips of bacon on the top.

To make a simple pâté you usually use ground pork instead of beef (much more flavor when cooked an hour or more), often pork liver (which adds greater dimension to the flavor), ground veal (it lightens things), and always at least a third the weight of those meats in ground pork fat (a lot more than in hamburger), which not only adds taste but also helps keep the pâté moist. If onions are added, they are usually sautéed for a few minutes beforehand to bring out their taste. Usually there is minced garlic as well, and often a tablespoon of good Cognac for, well, flavor! Both the meatloaf and the pâté usually contain an egg to help hold the ingredients together. But when a pâté is baked, it is always sealed in some manner (with layers of thinly sliced fat, or pastry, or simply just aluminum foil) so as to keep in the flavors. When it's done, a pâté is usually weighted down, often by simply putting a brick on it, which helps make it more compact and less crumbly when sliced. And it's allowed to sit at least overnight, to mature a bit, like a good wine. Meatloaves are generally served hot and pâtés usually at room temperature. Those are the chief differences.

Apart from the loaf pan, the only other piece of equipment needed to make most pâtés is either a food processor or a meat grinder to mince the meats. An inexpensive food mill with interchangeable discs is also helpful.

The rules for making pâtés are quite easy. Once you become familiar with them and have made a few, you'll be on your way to creating your own.

General Rules for Making Pâté

1. You need to line the mold or loaf pan with something to seal in the flavors while cooking. You may use pastry, very thin layers of pork fat, poultry skin or a clean, thin dishcloth soaked in warm lard and allowed to get cold. Or simply put your mixture in a well-buttered loaf pan and cover it tightly with aluminum foil.

Lining with pastry: Roll out the dough in a rectangle (remember to use quarter turns) to a ¼-inch thickness. Using the bottom of the pâté baking pan as a guide, cut out a rectangle of dough and reserve it for the lid of the pâté. Then cut out another rectangle large enough to cover the bottom of the pâté baking pan and the two long sides, with an overlap. Make certain that all corners are filled. Cut out two pieces for the remaining ends, extra long so that they too will overlap, about ½ inch.

Using water and a pastry or paint brush, paint the inside edges of the large piece of dough where it will be joined with the end pieces; then place the end pieces in the pan and press them to the large piece.

After filling the pastry in the usual way (see below) with or without a layer of fat, paint the overlapping edges of the pastry with water and fold them in, onto the pâté. Paint the top of the pastry with water, then put the reserved rectangle of pastry over it, pressing down gently.

Finally, take a fork and go all around the edges: About ¼ inch in from the edge of the pâté mold, insert the fork about ¼ inch into the pastry, then pull the tines of the fork toward the rim of the mold. This seals the pastry.

Paint the top layer of pastry with an egg wash—either a whole egg, beaten, or a yolk beaten with a little water. If you wish to add decorative bits of pastry, cut them out and place them on the pastry now, then paint their tops as well.

Finally, cut two or three small holes in the pastry and insert a small funnel in each to let the steam out as the pâté bakes. Small piping tubes for a pastry bag do very well, or you can make small funnel-cones from aluminum foil.

Lining with thin layers of pork fat: This is practical only if you know a specialty butcher who has one of the machines to cut this, as the ordinary butcher does not. You can buy the least lean salt pork available, or simply big chunks of pork fat, cut it into slices as thin as possible, then pound them *very* gently as if making veal scallops until they are about ⅛ inch thick. Line the mold as if you were using pastry.

Lining with a cloth: Simply take a piece of muslin, good cheesecloth, or a clean dish towel (not terry cloth) and cut it into a size large enough to completely wrap your loaf pan. Melt some lard and soak the cloth in it, then lay it on a baking or cooking sheet and refrigerate a bit till the fat cools. Use it like a piece of fat.

Lining with skin: If you are making a chicken, turkey, or duck pâté, you may carefully take off the skin and use it as a lining. The skin is mostly fat and will add excellent flavor to your pâté. Removing the skin is easy to do. Using a small knife and your fingers, start at the large open end and begin separating the skin from the flesh. You'll find it quite easy to get your fingers under the skin, so just keep poking and spreading the space between skin and flesh. Finally, make an incision down the bird's back. Pull the skin off, being careful to tear as little as possible. Around the wings the skin will usually have to be cut or torn. Around the drumsticks it can usually be simply pulled down and off once you have an opening around the larger part.

2. You need a "forcemeat" (ground meat filling) and, if you wish, a "salpicon." The forcemeat is usually pork, pork liver and veal, plus pork fat. Then add whatever other meat you are featuring, such as chicken, duck, etc. The meats are usually in equal proportions (1 cup ground

meat equals about ½ pound), and one-third the weight of all the meats is usually ground pork fat. The forcemeat is highly seasoned. Included often are sautéed chopped onion, minced garlic, Cognac and salt—the general rule being 1 teaspoon of seasoning per pound (2 cups) of fat and meats. Something is also required to help bind the pâté and keep it from crumbling, usually an egg, or an egg and a little flour, or gelatin.

The "salpicon" adds interest and texture. This is strips of meat, usually thick, sometimes strips of fat, and often nuts or truffles. In forming the pâté you place a layer of forcemeat, then a layer of strips, another of forcemeat, and so on, ending with forcemeat. When the pâté is sliced it looks like a mosaic.

Forming and Baking the Pâté

The pâté can be baked in several ways, and each way gives it a different name.

PÂTÉ: Classically this implies "in pastry." The word *pâté* comes from the same source as pasta and pastry, and a hamburger "patty" is an English word of the same derivation, now slightly changed from its original meaning. A real pâté should be sealed in pastry and baked; to call something a "pâté en croûte" (pâté in pastry) is technically redundant but is certainly correct in today's language. Pâtés may be served hot or at room temperature, but never cold.

TERRINE: This is a pâté baked without pastry, in a loaf pan. It is also the name of the loaf pan, from the Latin *terra* ("earth"), referring to the earthenware originally used to bake pâtés in. Terrines should be served hot or at room temperature.

GALANTINE: This is fowl or veal that has been boned and stuffed with a forcemeat, usually cooked in its own skin, wrapped like a large sausage in a double layer of cheesecloth, and poached. It is served cold, often in its own aspic.

BALLOTINE: This is a type of galantine of meat, game, poultry or fish, usually served hot. But the word is often used interchangeably with galantine.

PANTIN: This is a pâté en croûte baked out of a loaf pan, sort of a free-standing pâté.

MOUSSE: The word simply means "foamy" and applies to more than chocolate. In the realm of pâtés it's a finely sieved mixture of liver, poultry or fish, bound with eggs and cooked in a terrine or soufflé dish in a water bath.

To confuse things even more, sometimes pâtés are not officially cooked at all. Some use sautéed liver, pureed with fat, seasoned and placed in a dish, or perhaps leftover cooked meats, puréed with fat and seasoned. An example would be the Smoked Salmon Pâté in this book.

Cooking Pâté

Pâtés should be cooked slowly at a temperature no higher than 350 degrees, preferably in a water bath, to an internal temperature of 150 degrees. When poaching galantines or ballotines the water should be under 200 degrees, never at a boil.

Bake pâtés approximately 30 minutes per pound (about 2 cups of chopped meat). If the crust starts to burn, cover it with aluminum foil.

A pâté is cooked when a sharp knife comes out clean, when it's floating in its own fat, and when the fat juices are clear yellow with no rosy traces. At this point it should be removed from the oven, allowed to come to room temperature, weighted (I use a brick; a few cans will also do the trick nicely) to counter crumbling when sliced, and refrigerated at least overnight.

If you are making pâté en croûte, remove the pâté from the oven, let it cool about 15 minutes, then fill the empty spaces in the pâté with an aspic poured through the funnels. Let cool to room temperature. Then refrigerate at least 24 hours to set the aspic and develop full flavor.

Pâté Pastry (Pâte à Pâté)

Makes enough pastry for an 8-cup terrine

The pastry surrounding the forcemeat in a pâté is not meant to be eaten but, rather, to thoroughly seal everything together while baking. Not eating it is probably best for most of us, but if you can't resist, double the amount of butter for a better flavor. The pastry used is basically ordinary short pastry.

Cold flour	500 grams	1 pound	3½ cups
Salt	15 grams	1 teaspoon	1 teaspoon
Cold butter, diced	125 grams	4 ounces	8 tablespoons
Eggs	1 large	1 large	1 large
Ice water	2 deciliters	12-13 tablespoons	¾ cup

NOTE: *If you are using one column do not switch to another for other ingredients, as the columns are not exact equivalents.*

Place the cold flour in the bowl of a food processor fitted with a steel cutting blade. Add the salt and process by turning on and off.

Add the butter to the bowl. Turn the processor on and off 3 to 4 times, until the butter is cut into the flour in about the size of lima beans—not too small.

Mix the egg and ice water together. With the processor running, add the mixture and process for approximately 5 seconds. *Do not wait until the dough forms a ball.* Remove from the bowl and put in a plastic bag, quickly press it together into a disc (ready for rolling out) and refrigerate for at least 2 hours. Do not seal the bag tightly; let it breathe a bit.

Seasonings for Pâtés

In making pâtés there are certain basic seasonings that reappear regularly and are staple items in most French kitchens. The most widely used are *Quatre Épices* (Four Spices), *Épices Fines* (Fine Spices) and *Sel Épicé* (Spiced Salt). A bottled variety of Quatre Épices is found in virtually every French supermarket. Most spices are best when freshly ground and lose strength when they have sat on the shelf too long. (Salt is an obvious exception.) However, it is a good idea to make a quantity of at least Four Spices and have it on hand; it can be used for seasoning many foods such as hamburger or meatloaf, for instance.

Four Spices *(Quatre Épices)*

The four spices are officially pepper, cloves, ginger and nutmeg. Sometimes cinnamon is included or substituted for the ginger. In France the official mixture is 125 grams of pepper, 10 grams of cloves, 30 grams of ginger and 35 grams of nutmeg. A rough approximation by volume measurement is 7 parts pepper to 1 part each of the other three spices.

2 teaspoons freshly ground pepper, preferably white
¼ teaspoon ground cloves
¼ teaspoon ground ginger
¼ teaspoon ground nutmeg

Mix all the ingredients together and store in a tightly closed jar.

Spiced Salt (Sel Épicé)

Spiced salt is exactly what its name implies. In a recipe calling for salt and Four Spices this could be substituted. The simple formula is 5 parts salt to 1 part pepper and 1 part "mixed spices," every chef having his own special variety.

5 teaspoons fine salt
1 teaspoon freshly ground pepper
1 teaspoon Four Spices

Mix all the ingredients together and store in a tightly closed jar.

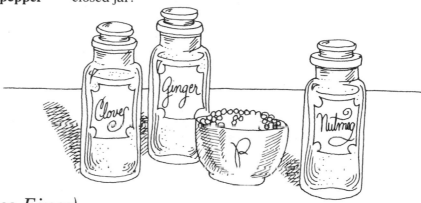

Fine Spices (Épices Fines)

This is a more sophisticated and professional version of Four Spices. Given below are the official quantities in grams, and a good volume equivalent (not exactly the same).

50 grams (1 tablespoon) bay
  leaves
50 grams (1 tablespoon) ground
  cloves
100 grams (1 tablespoon) mace
50 grams (1 tablespoon) nutmeg
300 grams (1 tablespoon) paprika
50 grams (1½ teaspoons)
  cinnamon
50 grams (1½ teaspoons)
  marjoram
50 grams (1½ teaspoons) sage
50 grams (1½ teaspoons) savory
50 grams (1½ teaspoons)
  rosemary
700 grams (½ cup) white
  peppercorns

Pulverize all the ingredients thoroughly, then strain. Store in a tightly closed jar.

TO PULVERIZE: You can begin by using a food processor or blender, but you may have trouble with the bay leaves. An electric coffee grinder used only for grinding spices (otherwise you'll pick up a coffee flavor) is perhaps the best available instrument for pulverizing spices.

Savory Pâtés

Rillettes

Makes 6 cups

Rillettes (pronounced rhee-ette) are a French favorite just being discovered in America. They make wonderful Christmas gifts, keep for months, refrigerated, and are good to have on hand to provide an excellent hors d'oeuvre at a moment's notice. They're potted in little jars or ramekins, allowed to come to room temperature, then used as a spread on crisp pieces of toast. Serve them as a first course by passing them in a dish along with little cornichons (sour pickles), which balance their richness.

Get the cheapest cut of pork; I generally use shoulder. The cooking is simplicity itself; the only difficult part is the shredding of the meat. I take great pleasure in working with my hands on such tasks, which I find relaxing. Shredding can be done in a food processor, but the texture is not nearly so good, and you miss the fun.

2 pounds leaf lard (pork kidney fat)
4 pounds pork shoulder
½ cup water
4 tablespoons salt
2 cloves garlic, minced
1 teaspoon leaf thyme
Freshly ground pepper
1-2 teaspoons Fine Spices
(see page 65)

Preheat the oven to 250 degrees.

Melt the lard in a cooking vessel large enough to hold all the meat. Meanwhile cut the pork into 2-inch cubes. Add the pork and the water (to keep it from sticking) and cook at least 4 hours, covered, either on top of the stove over very low heat or in the oven. The fat must not be boiling, only barely simmering. Cook until the meat is meltingly tender. Strain the pork from the fat, pressing down gently on the pork and reserving each separately.

Shred the pork by hand, pulling the individual meat fibers

apart. Place in a pan, add salt, garlic, and spices, and cook about 10 minutes to distribute the seasonings.

Mash the pork into small baking dishes with enough fat to form a sort of paste. Melt some of the separated cooking fat, but do *not* use the meat juices, to cover and seal each dish. Cover with aluminum foil and refrigerate. To serve, remove from refrigerator and let come to room temperature, about 2 hours.

Rillons

Makes 6 cups

Rillons (pronounced rhee-own) are much the same as rillettes but are rarely seen because they sell as fast as they're put on display—in France, which is the only place that you're likely to find them. They make excellent cocktail fare, especially for a party where hors d'oeuvres are passed. Simply stick toothpicks into them and watch them disappear. Rillons and rillettes may be started in the same pot; you might turn half the meat into rillettes and half into rillons.

2 pounds leaf lard (pork kidney fat)
4 pounds pork shoulder
½ cup water

Preheat the oven to 250 degrees.

Melt the lard in a cooking vessel large enough to hold all the meat. Cut the pork into 2-inch cubes. Add the pork cubes and water to the lard and cook a good 4 hours, covered, either on top of the stove over low heat or in the oven. Raise the oven temperature to 350 degrees, uncover the vessel (or put it on top of the stove) and watch the rillons carefully. As soon as they are a crusty, golden brown all over, drain them—do not let them burn. Serve at room temperature.

NOTE: If you wish to store the rillons, pour a little lard into the bottom of a glass jar and chill to firm; then fill the jar with rillons almost to the top; finally pour in more lard (not too hot) to fill and seal the jar. Put the top on and refrigerate. To use, gently reheat the jar in the oven until the lard is liquid enough to permit you to remove the rillons. Reheat them in an open pan and serve hot or at room temperature.

Tuna or Salmon Pâté

This pâté is quite simple to make and provides a lovely hors d'oeuvre for tuna lovers. This falls in the realm of uncooked pâtés, which use previously cooked foodstuffs recycled in new ways. They should appeal to beginning cooks and those who find the whole idea of pâtés rather fearsome. They should also appeal to cooks with limited time as well as to anyone who likes simple, honest food.

Select a good canned tuna or salmon, preferably not packed in water. Sardines or other canned fish may also be substituted. While it is not entirely necessary to use the food mill, it is impossible to obtain the fine texture without it.

6½- or 7-ounce can of tuna or salmon
6 tablespoons unsalted butter, at room temperature
1-1½ tablespoons freshly squeezed lemon juice
Freshly ground pepper
½ cup heavy cream, very cold
2 tablespoons minced fresh chives or capers
1 tablespoon minced fresh parsley (optional, but should be used if using capers)

Drain the tuna, discarding the oils or water. Place in a food processor or blender with the butter and process until it is a smooth paste; you may have to scrape it down occasionally. Add the lemon juice, a few turns of the pepper mill, process again to mix and then taste for seasoning; it should be highly seasoned as the whipped cream will dilute the strength.

Beat the cream in a chilled bowl till it has doubled in volume and "tracks" are left from the whisk or beater but the peaks will still flow when the bowl is tilted. With a rubber spatula, fold the cream into the tuna mixture.

Pass the pâté through the finest blade of a food mill, then fold in the chives or capers and parsley.

Pack the pâté into a serving dish or mound it on a small attractive plate. Refrigerate about 2 hours to firm.

Serve this pâté with small slices of toast, crusts removed, and a kir or nice California Riesling before dinner or lunch.

Smoked Salmon Pâté with Caviar

This extremely simple pâté is now almost a classic in nouvelle cuisine restaurants. It takes a very short time to make. In this recipe, it is imperative that you use a food mill or, even better, a tamis, a French drum sieve. It takes a certain amount of effort to press the mixture through the fine mesh, but this is how you achieve the delicate texture that is so important.

½ pound smoked salmon
1 cup crème fraîche or heavy cream
½ ounce caviar, black or red

Puree the salmon in a food processor, leaving it on for several minutes in order to get as fine a texture as possible.

If using crème fraîche, whip it lightly; if using heavy cream, beat it to the soft-peak stage.

Fold the cream into the salmon, then pass it through the

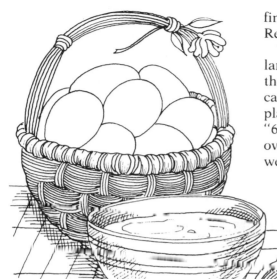

finest disc of a food mill, or preferably through a fine tamis. Refrigerate about 1 hour to firm.

To serve, take 2 teaspoons and dip them in water. Scoop a large walnut-sized portion of salmon pâté with one spoon, then, using the second, pat it to form it into an oval. If you can, slide the oval from spoon to spoon once or twice. Then place the oval on a plate (3 or 4 on a serving plate in the "2," "6," and "10" positions of a clock face). On the top of each oval place a small amount of caviar. Garnish with lemon wedges and serve with slices of brioche or toast.

Italian Veal and Prosciutto Terrine

Serves 12

This exceedingly simple terrine is both unusual and delicious. It was given to me by Jo Bettoja, who runs the Lo Scaldavivande Cooking School in Rome with her friend Anna-Maria Cornetto. When they came to New York and gave classes in my school, this was one of the home recipes she used. Its remarkable simplicity and elegant taste make it perfect for someone who has never made a pâté.

If you cannot find veal in your market (most veal sold in America is really baby beef, which you can always tell by its red color; veal is a very pale, grayish pink), then use pork instead. Be sure you have an excellent quality Parmesan cheese, preferably Reggiano or the American-produced Asiago.

8 large eggs
½ teaspoon freshly ground pepper
3 ounces Parmesan cheese, freshly grated
1 pound veal (for scaloppine), thinly sliced, pounded thinner if necessary
7 ounces mortadella, sliced thinly
7 ounces prosciutto, sliced very thinly

Preheat the oven to 350 degrees.

Beat the eggs with the pepper and cheese. Dip slices of veal in the egg mixture and make a layer on the bottom of a 6- to 8-cup loaf pan. Cover with a layer of mortadella, also dipped in egg, then with prosciutto dipped in egg, continuing until you end with a layer of veal. Pour in any extra egg mixture but do not cover the top layer of veal.

Put the loaf pan in a larger baking dish, surround it with boiling water, and cook in the oven for 2 hours.

Let cool to room temperature; unmold if you wish. Cut thick slices and garnish with sprigs of parsley.

Express Chicken Liver Pâté

This rich and delicious spread is simple to prepare and makes an elegant and auspicious beginning for a memorable meal. Don't limit yourself to chicken livers; the livers from ducks, Rock Cornish game hens, or any other fowl can be used. Livers can vary in color greatly, from yellowish to deep burgundy. I always save my chicken livers, putting them into a little jar in the freezer until there are enough to use. I also freeze duck livers if I'm not using them. A combination of livers from various fowls is also excellent. Of course you can cut the recipe in half if you have only ½ pound of livers.

1 pound chicken livers
8 tablespoons unsalted butter
2 tablespoons Armagnac or Cognac
3 tablespoons port, Madeira or
**   sherry**
1 clove garlic, finely minced
1½ teaspoons salt
Freshly ground pepper
Four Spices or Fine Spices (see
**   pages 64 and 65) to taste**

Carefully pick over the livers, removing any fat, green particles or extraneous bits.

Melt 2 to 3 tablespoons of butter over medium heat in a sauté pan, then cook the livers 3 to 4 minutes until they are stiffened but still quite pink on the inside. Put the livers in a blender or food processor and process to a fine paste.

Add the Armagnac or Cognac to the sauté pan and cook 1 minute; add the port and cook another minute, scraping up any residue from the livers. Add this to the food processor with all the remaining ingredients, including the remaining butter and process briefly to mix well. Taste for seasoning and add the spices if needed.

Scrape the mixture into a serving dish and refrigerate about 2 hours to firm. Serve cold with toast, crusts removed. It's very rich, so butter won't be necessary.

NOTE: Put this pâté in a jar with a little melted lard poured over the top to seal it, and it will keep a good 3 weeks refrigerated.

Country-Style Pâté

This delicious pâté is one we do in our classes, and it always wins lots of praise. It's a coarse, chunky pâté, garlicky and hearty, rich with flavor, typical of the pâté one finds in a small French family-run restaurant.

If you can get your butcher to grind the meats for you, making this will be simplicity itself. It's better if the meat is ground in a meat grinder rather than in a food processor because it will have more texture. Best yet is to chop it by hand, but that's a great deal of work. Use pork liver if you possibly can—its fine flavor makes so much difference that it might even be considered the "secret ingredient."

8 ounces fresh pork, ground
8 ounces fresh pork fat, ground
8 ounces lean veal or chuck, ground
8 ounces pork liver
1 tablespoon unsalted butter
6 tablespoons chopped onion
1 large egg
2 tablespoons Armagnac or Cognac
3 cloves garlic, minced
1 teaspoon Four Spices (see page 64)
  or ½ bay leaf ground with
  ¾ teaspoon thyme
1-2 tablespoons salt
½ teaspoon freshly ground pepper
1 tablespoon flour
10 ounces pork fat to line mold,
  sliced very thin
4 ounces ham in ¼-inch slices, then
  cut in ¼-inch strips

Mix all the ground meats and fat together in a large bowl with your hands. Liquify the liver in a food processor or blender, add it to the meats and mix again.

Melt the butter and sauté the onion about 5 minutes, until translucent but not browned. Add to the bowl along with the egg, Armagnac, garlic, spices, salt and pepper. Sprinkle the flour over all and mix well again. Take a spoonful, shape it like a small hamburger and sauté it until cooked. Let cool, then taste for seasoning. It should be highly seasoned as when it is cooked and cooled the seasoning will diminish somewhat.

Line a 6-cup pâté mold with the lining fat, place a layer of a quarter of the forcemeat on the bottom, cover with a third of the ham strips, another quarter of the forcemeat, a third of the ham strips, continuing until all is used up and ending with a layer of forcemeat. Cover with the lining fat.

Preheat the oven to 350 degrees.

Cover the pâté mold (or use foil if you have no cover) and place it in a baking pan surrounded with boiling water. Carefully place in the oven and cook 1¼ to 1½ hours, or until the fat juices are clear yellow with no rosy traces. Discard water and cool to room temperature.

Weight and refrigerate at least 24 hours to develop its best flavor. Serve at room temperature, not cold, with sprigs of watercress around each slice (or with a pretty lettuce leaf) and a cornichon or two.

Duck Pâté

Duck pâté can be one of the best things that can happen to a duck, and to you. The good flavor of the bird is complemented by many different seasonings; here a hint of orange is used. The pâté makes excellent picnic fare or a fine hors d'oeuvre for an intimate dinner. You might even serve it for a festive evening buffet.

Fresh duckling will be better than frozen, but ducks freeze better than chickens. Just defrost very slowly, preferably in the refrigerator. If you reserve the skin of the duck, it will make an excellent lining for your mold, lending even more flavor, or you can render the fat from the skin and use it in place of lard to soak a clean cloth with which to line the mold.

4- to 5-pound duckling, skinned and boned
½ cup Grand Marnier or a good orange liqueur
1 teaspoon salt
½ teaspoon freshly ground pepper
1 teaspoon ground thyme
¼ cup minced fresh parsley
½ pound veal, ground
½ pound fatty pork, ground
1 large egg
Garnish: Fine julienne of orange rind, blanched 2 minutes (optional); watercress; cornichons

Either reserve the duck skin to line the mold or chop it up into large pieces, barely cover them with water in a saucepan and simmer to render the fat. When all the water is evaporated and the solid parts begin to splatter, it's done—strain and discard the solids and reserve the rendered fat.

Scrape the meat off the carcass. If you are lining the mold with pastry, save the bones for stock to form the aspic you will need (see Rabbit Pâté, page 78, for instructions). You should have a little more than 1 pound of duck meat. Take about 6-8 ounces of it (about half), preferably from the breast, and cut into thick strips. Toss them in a marinade of the Grand Marnier plus all the seasonings; cover and refrigerate overnight.

In a food processor using a steel blade, grind the rest of the duck meat, veal and pork together. Process at least 5 minutes, then pass through the medium disc of a food mill, to remove all sinewy, stringy pieces of duck.

Strain the refrigerated strips of duck and pour the marinade into a bowl together with the ground meats and the egg. Mix well.

Preheat the oven to 350 degrees.

In a lined 6-cup mold place a quarter of the forcemeat on the bottom, then a third of the duck strips, another quarter of the forcemeat, and so on until all is used up, ending with the forcemeat. Cover the top with lining fat (or skin, or a fat-drenched cloth, or fat and pastry), cover the mold and place in a baking dish with boiling water. Cook in the oven for 1½ to 2 hours or until the juices are clear.

Cool to room temperature, weight and refrigerate overnight. If you wish to keep the pâté, line it with a good ½ inch of duck fat or lard; it will keep many weeks like this if refrigerated.

To serve, let come to room temperature, cut ½-inch slices and garnish with blanched julienned orange rind, watercress and cornichons.

NOTE: If you are tired of the taste of duck with orange, use Madeira or port in place of the Grand Marnier and omit the julienne of orange rind.

Crisp Chicken or Turkey Pâté

Serves 8-10

If this pâté were wrapped in cheesecloth and poached, it would constitute a galantine, if served cold, or a ballotine, if eaten warm. But because it is baked in a loaf pan, it is a pâté. Unlike most pâtés this one is cooked with the cover left off, thus producing a rich, crisp skin encasing it. I recommend it for picnics and summer luncheons. Once you've made it, I'm sure it will become a standard in your repertory.

3- to 3½-pound chicken
6 ounces fatty pork, ground
6 ounces lean veal, ground
6 ounces pork fat, ground
6 ounces ham, ground
1 tablespoon salt
½ teaspoon freshly ground pepper
¼ teaspoon Fine Spices (see page 65)
¼ cup Armagnac or Cognac
2 large eggs
Skin of the chicken to line the mold or 10 ounces pork fat, thinly sliced

If you are lining the mold with the skin of the chicken, slip a finger between the flesh and the skin, starting at the large opening. You will find that the skin separates quite easily. Keep as much whole as you can.

Remove the breast meat of the chicken, cut it into large, thick strips and set aside. Remove and grind the rest of the chicken and the liver; if you are using a food processor, leave it on a good 5 minutes and then pass the ground chicken through the medium blade of a food mill to remove the many sinewy, stringy pieces. Mix it with the other ground meats and fats and stir in all the other ingredients except for the lining fat or skin. Sauté a small bit and taste for seasoning. It should be highly seasoned as serving it at room temperature will diminish the flavors.

Preheat the oven to 350 degrees.

Line the pâté mold with the skin or fat. Put a quarter of the forcemeat on the bottom of the lined mold, then a third of the breast strips, and continue until all is used up, ending with a layer of forcemeat. Top with the skin or lining fat. Place in a baking pan uncovered, surround with boiling water, and place in the oven. Cook 1¼ to 1½ hours, or until the juices are clear. Cool to room temperature, weight and refrigerate 24 hours.

Serve with a homemade Sauce Dijonnaise: mayonnaise with enough Dijon-style mustard to bring out its taste. It's also good with just Dijon mustard.

Herbed Chicken Galantine

Odette Sibony must be a very gifted cook, though I've yet to meet her. Her son Judah, who is one of Israel's most talented artists and a fine cook in his own right, taught me this elegant dish, which reflects Odette's fine sense of seasoning.

If boning a chicken puts you off, ask the butcher to do it, or buy chicken breasts and make the same recipe by simply wrapping the mixture in cheesecloth.

3½-pound chicken, skinned and
  boned
4 large eggs, 2 of them hardboiled
1 whole small nutmeg
Freshly ground white pepper
1 teaspoon salt
Pinch of cayenne pepper or drop
  of Tabasco
¾ cup minced fresh parsley
¼ cup heavy cream
Bouquet garni (parsley stems,
  ½ bay leaf, ½ teaspoon thyme,
  tied together in cheesecloth)
1 medium-size carrot, sliced in
  rounds
1 medium-size onion, sliced
1 stalk of celery, sliced

Skin and bone the chicken as described in the previous recipe. Put all of the meat except the liver in a food processor and grind it very finely. Add the eggs and process again.

Grate the whole nutmeg with a small grater and put it, with the pepper, salt, cayenne pepper, parsley and cream, into the processor bowl. Turn on for a few seconds to blend evenly. Chop the liver and stir it in.

Put several layers of cheesecloth on a work surface, then place the chicken skin on the cheesecloth "on its back." Put the chicken mixture on the skin in a long sausage-like strip, then cover it with the skin and tie the cheesecloth over it to form a large sausage. Tie the two ends (there may not be any skin covering the ends), but don't roll it too tight.

Put the chicken bones in a pot large enough to hold the galantine, add water just to cover, put in the bouquet garni and the aromatic vegetables and bring to the simmer. Add the chicken and poach for 1½ hours.

Remove the chicken from the poaching liquid and let cool 2 days in the refrigerator in the cheesecloth. To increase the flavor of the poaching liquid, you may reduce it by boiling it down. Then clarify it with egg white and turn it into an aspic formed on a baking sheet. Cut the aspic into "diamonds" by cutting diagonals, then lifting them off with a metal spatula. Place around the slices of galantine.

Veal Ballotine with Zucchini Farce

Serves 8-10

This easy ballotine utilizes zucchini to lighten the stuffing, an idea suggested by Richard Olney.
It couldn't be easier to bone a breast of veal, but if you have any qualms, ask your butcher to do it for you.
The object is simply to have a big piece of flat meat which can envelop a stuffing.

1 pound zucchini
1 teaspoon salt
1 lemon, zested and juiced
5-pound veal breast, boned, with
    bones reserved
8 tablespoons unsalted butter
6 tablespoons minced shallots
¾ pound fatty pork, finely ground
1 large egg, beaten
1 teaspoon Fine Spices or Four
    Spices (see pages 64 and 65)
1 teaspoon dried tarragon
1 carrot, scraped and sliced
1 medium-size onion, peeled and
    sliced
1 stalk celery, sliced
3 cups veal or chicken stock
1-2 cups dry white wine
Bouquet garni (parsley stems,
    ½ bay leaf, ½ teaspoon thyme,
    tied together in cheesecloth)
1 cup heavy cream or crème fraîche

Preheat the oven to 325 degrees.

Wash the zucchini well to remove all grit. Cut off the ends, then grate by hand or in a food processor. Toss with the salt and place in a sieve to drain off juices for 20 to 30 minutes.

Sprinkle the lemon juice over the veal and let sit up to 2 hours. More lemon juice may be used if needed.

Melt the butter in a large skillet over medium heat, add the shallots and cook for 2 to 3 minutes, until translucent but not brown.

Squeeze the zucchini with your hands to remove as much water as possible. Then add it to the shallots and cook over medium heat for 2 to 3 minutes, until fairly dry. Place in a mixing bowl together with the lemon zest, pork, beaten egg, spices and tarragon, and mix well. Take 1 tablespoon of the farce, make a little hamburger and sauté until well cooked; taste and adjust seasoning.

Spread the veal out on a double layer of cheesecloth and put the farce over the veal, leaving the top third free. Then bring the top and bottom of the veal together, forming a large sausage. Using a large upholstery needle and string, sew the top and bottom of the veal together. Then wrap the cheesecloth tightly around it, securing the two ends with string. Loosely tie the "sausage" in three or four places.

Place the bones, aromatic vegetables, stock, wine and bouquet garni in a cooking vessel large enough to hold the veal ballotine, and bring to the boil. Place the ballotine in the liquid. If it isn't covered with liquid, add enough water to do so, bring to the simmer, and place in the oven for 2 hours.

Remove the veal from the cooking vessel, take off the cheesecloth and place the veal on a warm platter covered with aluminum foil.

Strain the cooking juices, degrease them and finally reduce to 2 cups or less. Add the cream or crème fraîche and reduce to 2 cups. Taste for seasoning, then use as a sauce over slices of the ballotine.

(continued)

NOTE: This may also be served at room temperature (never refrigerator cold), but it should then be referred to as a galantine. Degrease and reduce the cooking liquids, but instead of adding the cream, clarify and turn into an aspic to garnish the cold slices. A homemade green mayonnaise would be excellent as a sauce.

Turkey Ballotine with
Maple-Glazed Chestnuts

Serves 10-12

This recipe was given to me by Antoine Bouterin, a good friend and fine chef, formerly of the celebrated Parisian restaurant Au Quai D'Orsay and currently chef at the Périgord in New York City. He comes from the south of France and cooks in the lusty style of that region.

This is what I call a "turn the page" recipe, because it appears so complicated or difficult that most people turn the page when they read it to look for something easier. In reality it is not difficult. It can and should be made ahead of time and is the perfect solution for a Thanksgiving dinner that you must do ahead and one where you don't want to walk away from the table feeling as stuffed as the turkey.

Using a large turkey breast makes the most difficult part of the recipe quite easy. Use very good chestnuts and of course a fine Armagnac or Cognac, not a cheap brandy. With good ingredients you'll find it difficult to go wrong, and this becomes a very tasty dish, not only for Thanksgiving but for any festive occasion.

4-5 pound turkey or turkey breast
¾ cup Armagnac or Cognac
2 teaspoons salt
1 teaspoon freshly ground pepper
4 tablespoons minced fresh parsley
2 teaspoons dried tarragon
1 tablespoon minced fresh chives
10 ounces fatty pork
½ cup minced shallots
1 clove garlic, minced
5 ounces breadcrumbs
1 cup heavy cream or crème fraîche
5 ounces sausage meat (sweet rather
    than hot or spicy)
2 large eggs
12 ounces peeled chestnuts, Faugier
    brand if you can find them
4 cups turkey or chicken stock
½ cup maple syrup
2 cups freshly made cranberry sauce

Bone the turkey, carefully removing the skin so as to have as few holes as possible and removing as much of the meat as you can. If using a large turkey breast, which is much easier, follow the same procedure. Marinate the skin 4 to 5 hours in 3 to 4 tablespoons of the brandy, half the salt and pepper, 1 tablespoon of the parsley and half the tarragon and chives.

Chop the turkey meat (or use a food processor) with the pork, shallots, garlic and the remainder of the salt and pepper. Soak the breadcrumbs in the cream, then mix all the meats with the breadcrumbs, sausage, remaining herbs, eggs and the rest of the brandy. Let the mixture rest, refrigerated, for several hours or, better, overnight.

Preheat the oven to 325 degrees.

Spread the turkey skin out on its back on a larger piece of cheesecloth. Place half of the forcemeat on the skin lengthwise in a strip about 10 inches long and 4 inches wide, place a row of chestnuts down the center of the stuffing and cover them with the rest of the mixture. Wrap the mixture up in the turkey skin like a long sausage and wrap that in the cheesecloth, tying the ends with string so that it won't come apart when cooking.

Bring the turkey stock to a simmer in a large pan, place the ballotine in it, add any turkey bones and cook in the oven about 2½ hours.

Let the ballotine cool to room temperature before taking it from the liquid and carefully removing the cheesecloth. Serve ¾-inch slices garnished with the rest of the chestnuts glazed in maple syrup; pass cranberry sauce on the side.

NOTE: To glaze the chestnuts, place them in a saucepan with the maple syrup and cook over low heat until they begin to brown and glaze, about 15 to 20 minutes. You may have to add a tablespoon of water from time to time to keep them from burning. For cranberry sauce, use your favorite recipe or follow the directions on the cranberry package; add 1 to 2 tablespoons of Grand Marnier or another good orange liqueur for better flavor.

Rabbit Pâté

Rabbit pâté is one of the great classics, and deservedly so, for its fine flavor comes through even when the rabbit is battery-raised. This is a pâté designed to win raves from your guests, to be served on a special occasion.

The pâté can, of course, be done as a terrine; simply wrap the rabbit in thin layers of pork fat instead of pastry. But if you wish to present this pâté in all its glory, take several days to make it, breaking the process down into several simple steps. While it's best to use a freshly killed rabbit, rabbit freezes quite well. If the boning puts you off, have your butcher do it for you.

1 recipe of pâté dough (see page 63)
3-4 pound rabbit
¾ pound veal
¾ pound pork
3 tablespoons olive oil
3 tablespoons minced fresh parsley
2 medium-size onions, sliced
1 medium-size carrot, sliced
2 cloves garlic, minced
¾ cup dry white wine
2 tablespoons Armagnac or Cognac
1 teaspoon salt
1 stalk celery, sliced
Bouquet garni (fresh parsley stems, ¼ teaspoon leaf thyme, ½ bay leaf, tied in cheesecloth)
1 egg yolk beaten with 1 tablespoon water
2 packages unflavored gelatin
2-3 tablespoons Madeira or port
2-3 egg whites and their shells (optional)

Make the pâté dough and refrigerate it for 1 or 2 days before using it.

Bone the rabbit: Use a small, sharp knife and scrape the bones, keeping as much as possible in whole pieces for the salpicon from the loin and legs. Cut 3 to 4 ounces of this meat into thick strips and do the same with one third of the veal and one third of the pork. Prepare a marinade for the strips to soak in overnight with the oil, parsley, one third of the onions, half the carrots, garlic, ¼ cup of the wine and 1 tablespoon Cognac.

In a food processor mince the remaining rabbit meat with the heart and liver. Add the remaining veal and pork and process until very smooth. To remove any stringy fibers, pass through the medium blade of a food mill. Mix this forcemeat with the remaining wine, Cognac and salt. Place half the remaining onions over it and let it sit, refrigerated, overnight.

With the rabbit bones prepare a stock: Boil in water to cover for 2 to 3 hours, add the remaining carrot, onion, celery and bouquet garni and immediately turn the fire off and cover. After 15 minutes strain, cool, then refrigerate. NOTE: For a better-tasting stock, begin by browning the bones, either by sautéing in butter or by roasting in the oven.

Preheat the oven to 350 degrees.

Line a 6-cup pâté mold with the dough. Place a layer of forcemeat on the bottom, then a layer of the strips of the three meats, next another layer of forcemeat, and so on, ending with a layer of forcemeat. With a brush, paint the overlapping pastry with water, then turn it over the pâté; cover with the rectangle of pastry, seal with the tines of a fork, paint with the beaten egg yolk, then add any decorative bits and paint them as well. Make vent holes and insert foil funnels (or use pastry tips). Bake in a water bath for 1½ hours, or until the juices in the funnels are clear. Remove from the waterbath and let cool to room temperature.

Meanwhile make the aspic: Skim any fat off the top of the chilled rabbit stock. Taste for flavor and boil down to 2 cups or less to intensify the flavor if needed.

For each cup of stock, moisten 1 package of gelatin in 1 to 2 tablespoons of Madeira. Add to the stock.

Heat the stock to the simmering point as you beat the egg whites with the shells, until frothy. Then add to the stock. Stir till it comes to a bare simmer; then, without stirring, let it barely simmer 10 to 15 minutes. Turn off the heat and let cool about 10 minutes. Carefully pour through a paper-napkin-lined strainer (*not* filter paper or paper towels, as they're too thick), trying not to disturb the egg whites. If the stock is not clear, repeat the egg-white process in this paragraph with additional egg whites. Then cool until syrupy.

While the pate is still warm and in its mold, fill the spaces caused by the shrinking of the meat by pouring aspic in the funnels. Any remaining aspic may be poured onto a baking sheet and refrigerated to set. Before serving, cut diagonal lines in two directions, then with a flexible metal spatula lift up the resulting "diamonds" of aspic and place them around the pâté on the serving platter.

The pâté should be refrigerated at least 2 days to develop flavor. Remove from the mold and place on a platter. Slice one or two thirds of it laying one slice over another, leading up to the uncut portion. Garnish with watercress, extra aspic as described above and cornichons. Serve at room temperature for full flavor.

Nouvelle Cuisine Vegetable Terrine

This delicious vegetable terrine is based on one introduced by the Troisgros brothers at their excellent three-star restaurant in Roanne, a small, nondescript town in the middle of France. This was probably the dish that first popularized vegetable terrines, and in my opinion it remains one of the best. It is a perfect first course for a summer dinner outdoors and can be made several days ahead.

I've seen versions of this dish made with chicken or turkey instead of ham, but they lose the great character that the original has. The Troisgros brothers use truffles in theirs, but apart from the unconscionable price of such truffles as we can buy in America, the overwhelming majority are so tasteless that there is virtually no reason for buying them in the first place. You may substitute any vegetables that will hold up in the cooking process for those used here.

**6 ounces red bell peppers
(pimientos) or tiny young green
beans**
**5 ounces (½ package) frozen
baby peas**
**2 medium-size cucumbers or
zucchini**
10 ounces small new carrots, peeled
½ lemon
1 tablespoon butter
1½ pounds smoked ham
10 vine leaves
2 lemons, juiced
¼ teaspoon freshly ground pepper
2 large eggs
1 cup safflower oil, chilled
Cold Tomato Sauce (see below)

Scorch the skins of the peppers over a gas burner or under the broiler for about 6 to 8 minutes, then place them in a plastic bag for a few minutes. Remove the outer skins, ribs and cores under cold running water. Cut into fine julienne strips. If using green beans, blanch them in salted boiling water until they are barely tender. Chill.

Defrost the peas by leaving the package out or by running cold water over them. Peel the cucumbers and scoop out the seeds. (If you are using zucchini, merely scrub them and cut off the ends; do not seed.) Cut the cucumbers or zucchini and carrots into lengthwise quarters. Blanch the vegetables in salted boiling water until tender. Chill.

Place the bowl of the food processor in the freezer. Cut the ham into small dice and place in the freezer for 30 minutes.

Preheat the oven to 325 degrees. Rinse the vine leaves and use them to line a 6- to 8-cup loaf pan, overlapping the leaves.

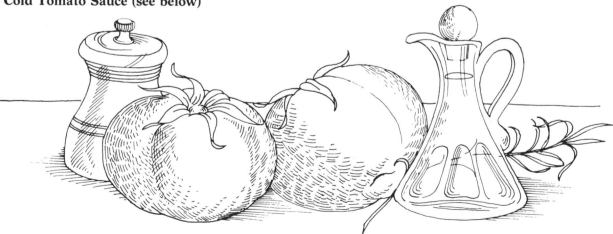

Place the chilled ham, lemon juice and pepper in the cold bowl of the food processor and process briefly. Add the eggs and, when they are well blended, add the cold oil in a thin, slow stream as though making mayonnaise.

Make sure all the vegetables are dry and cold. Place a layer of ham in the lined pan, then a layer of carrots, a layer of ham, a layer of peas, another layer of ham, then a layer of cucumbers or zucchini, a layer of ham, a layer of red peppers and, finally, a layer of ham. Fold the vine leaves over the top and cover with buttered wax paper. Place the loaf pan in a pan of boiling water and cook for 45 to 60 minutes. Let it cool in the bain marie out of the oven, then chill a minimum of 8 hours before unmolding (this is very important).

To serve, pour a ladle of the tomato sauce on a chilled plate. Place a 1-inch slice of the terrine, including the vine leaves, on the sauce-covered plate, garnish with leftover julienned peppers or green beans.

COLD TOMATO SAUCE

1½ cups sauce

1½ pounds vine-ripened tomatoes
1½ teaspoons tomato paste
4 teaspoons red wine vinegar
¼ cup imported olive oil
½ teaspoon salt
¼ teaspoon freshly ground pepper
1 tablespoon minced tarragon or basil
2 tablespoons minced fresh parsley

Drop tomatoes into boiling water for 15 to 25 seconds, remove and peel. Cut in half horizontally and squeeze out the seeds. Chop roughly, then pass through the finest blade of a food mill. Refrigerate.

Just before serving, add the tomato paste and vinegar to the puree and, whisking as if making mayonnaise, add the oil slowly. Season with salt, pepper, tarragon and parsley.

NOTE: If you are using dried tarragon, pour a little boiling water over it, let it sit a few minutes, then strain.

Summer Fruit Terrine

Serves 8-12

Fruit in pâtés is not a new idea, but it is one that has largely been forgotten. One of our last reminders is today's mincemeat pie; the apple pie is also derivative. For our dessert pâtés we will have terrines, baked without pastry. This one uses banana for the forcemeat, combined with farmer's cheese to give it more body. When you slice it through and see the rich mosaic of seasonal fruits, it will remind you of a "true" pâté.

Look for bananas with "freckles," which denote ripeness and perfection. For the other fruits, select a variety of the ripest available and poach them in a light syrup. Berries should not be poached and must be very firm.

4-5 ripe bananas
8 ounces farmer's cheese
2 large eggs
¾ cup plus 2 tablespoons sugar
1 tablespoon dark rum
¼ teaspoon cinnamon
1 each of 3 or 4 varieties of fruits:
  peaches, nectarines or apricots;
  plums; papayas or mangoes;
  1 cup of strawberries, raspberries,
  blueberries or seedless grapes
Fresh mint sprigs

Preheat the oven to 350 degrees.

Peel the bananas and puree them in a food processor together with the cheese, eggs, 2 tablespoons of sugar, rum and cinnamon. Set aside in a bowl.

Prepare a poaching syrup with 2 cups of water and the rest of the sugar; bring to a boil, turn down the heat and simmer for 4 to 5 minutes. Peel the fruit by dropping into boiling water for 15 to 30 seconds. Reserve the skins. Cut into quarters and poach in the syrup, one fruit after another, until tender. This will take from 3 to 12 minutes, depending upon the ripeness of the fruit. When all the fruit is poached except the berries, return the reserved peelings to the syrup and reduce

by half to two-thirds until thick and syrupy. Strain and discard peelings.

In a buttered 6-cup mold put a quarter of the banana forcemeat, then a layer of one fruit in slices; cover with another quarter of the forcemeat, then a layer of another fruit, continuing until you finish with a layer of forcemeat. Cover the mold with buttered aluminum foil and bake for 45 to 60 minutes, or until done, in a baking pan surrounded with boiling water. Cool to room temperature, then refrigerate.

To serve, put some of the syrup on the plate and spread it all around; place a slice of the terrine in the center and decorate with a sprig of fresh mint.

NOTE: A lighter, more delicate version may be made by omitting the farmer's cheese and using 1 cup of heavy cream, whipping it to stiff peaks and carefully folding it into the banana mixture. In this case a tablespoon of flour added to the banana mixture is needed for a firmer setting. Or, save the fruit syrup for another use and serve a Vanilla Custard Sauce, flavored with rum, kirsch or another fruit alcohol.

VANILLA CUSTARD SAUCE

3 large eggs
½ cup sugar
2 teaspoons flour
2 cups hot milk
2-3 teaspoons vanilla or liqueur
2-4 tablespoons unsalted butter

Beat the eggs with the sugar in a 2-quart saucepan until they are pale yellow and form a ribbon. Beat in the flour and stir well. Immediately add the hot milk and, stirring, bring just to the boil; immediately remove the pan from the heat and stir continuously until somewhat cooled. Add the vanilla and/or optional liqueur to taste; you may add butter for additional flavor and richness.

Winter Fruit Terrine
Serves 8-12

According to the Larousse, *France's encyclopedia of cookery, dessert pâtés were once made using pastry cream in place of the forcemeat. In this winter version we use frangipane, or pastry cream which incorporates pulverized almonds. This heartier version is quite delicious, and the winter fruits are set forth with distinction.*

The banana is used once again, this time as part of the salpicon, together with fruits of fall and winter: pears, apples and dried prunes. To poach fruits is to elevate them to new heights and provides a surprise for fugitives from canned fruit cocktail. Poached bananas are especially good. You should try them with ice cream for a very special banana split.

4 large eggs
2¼ cups sugar
1 cup all-purpose flour
2 cups milk, very hot
6 tablespoons unsalted butter
1 tablespoon vanilla
¼ teaspoon almond extract
1 cup almonds, blanched
¾ cup dried, pitted prunes
4 tablespoons Madeira or port
2 apples, Granny Smith if possible
2 pears
2 bananas
8 ounces apricot jam

Beat the eggs and 1½ cups of sugar with a hand mixer in a bowl until they are very light yellow and creamy. Add the flour and continue beating to incorporate well without lumps. Put in a saucepan, add the hot milk and bring to the boil while stirring. The mixture will get very thick. Turn the heat down and keep stirring for several minutes to cook the flour. Remove from the heat, add the butter, vanilla and almond extract and mix well.

In a food processor or blender, pulverize the almonds to a fine powder. Mix them into the pastry cream to form frangipane.

In a small saucepan cook the prunes in water to cover plus 1 to 2 tablespoons of wine until tender, about 8 minutes.

Make a poaching syrup of 2 cups of water and the remaining sugar; bring it to the boil, reduce the heat and simmer 4 to 5 minutes. Meanwhile peel the apples and pears, and core and quarter them. Poach the apples first, being very careful to take them out just as they become tender and before they turn to applesauce. Next poach the bananas, cut in length-wise halves or quarters; if ripe they will take about 3 to 4 minutes, if not as long as 10 to 15 minutes. Finally, poach the pears; depending on ripeness they may take anywhere from 4 minutes to 1 hour; just keep testing. When they are done, slice the apples and pears and cut the prunes in half lengthwise.

Preheat the oven to 350 degrees.

Fill the bottom of a buttered 6-cup mold with a fifth of the frangipane, then a layer of apples, then another fifth of the frangipane, then successive layers of prunes, frangipane, bananas, frangipane, pears, and finally a layer of frangipane. Cover the mold with foil, place in a baking pan filled with boiling water and cook in the oven for 45 minutes to 1 hour or until set. Let cool to room temperature.

Heat the apricot jam in a small saucepan with 2 tablespoons of water and 2 tablespoons of Madeira. Strain, pushing down on the fruit. To serve, cover the interior of individual plates with a thin coating of the sauce, place a slice of the terrine directly in the center, and place a piece of extra poached fruit on the center.